Praise for *Accelerate Your Career in Nursing*

"*Accelerate Your Career in Nursing* is not another 'how-to' book. It inspires and guides developing nurses by showcasing successful leaders' personal journeys and reflections on ways to develop self-awareness and self-sufficiency to build a rewarding career. Begin your journey by assembling an impressive portfolio, seeking colleagues who will help you gain recognition, and learning additional skills to achieve your personal best. Learn to be persuasive, bold, and fearless in preparing for the future."

–*Pamela F. Cipriano, PhD, RN, NEA-BC, FAAN*
Senior Director, Galloway Consulting Research
Associate Professor, University of Virginia School of Nursing
Editor-in-Chief, American Nurse Today

"A must-read book for those looking to advance in their career, professional association, and education. A true benefit that I wish had been available to me when climbing the corporate ladder!"

–*Jose Alejandro, PhD, MBA, RN-BC, CCM, FACHE*
Executive Director of Case Management, Steward Health Care System
Past President, National Association of Hispanic Nurses
Treasurer, Case Management Society of America

"This helpful book provides practical information for nurses who are considering professional advancement. It is well detailed on how to be successful in promoting nursing career changes and recognition for achievements. The presentation of real-life experiences of nurses seeking change adds clarification."

–*May L. Wykle, PhD, RN, FAAN, FGSA*
Dean & Professor Emeritus, Frances Payne Bolton School of Nursing,
Case Western Reserve University
President, Friends of the National Institute of Nursing Research
Past President, Sigma Theta Tau International

"The topics discussed in *Accelerate Your Career in Nursing* serve as an excellent guide to address the evidence-based recommendations of *The Future of Nursing: Leading Change, Advancing Health*, a 2011 report from the Institute of Medicine. It is both an honor and privilege to have available the wealth of wisdom that respected nursing leaders share in each chapter."

–John Lowe, PhD, RN, FAAN
Wymer Distinguished Professor
Christine E. Lynn College of Nursing
Florida Atlantic University

"Janice Phillips and Janet Boivin have put together a fantastic resource for students, new graduates, and experienced nurses who want to take hold of their career progression. The best part about this book is that it blends great wisdom and practical, easy-to-follow steps tailored to the nursing world. If you want to accelerate your career or make professional moves sooner, get this book!"

–Robert Fraser, MN, RN
Registered Nurse for General Internal Medicine,
University Health Network
Order Set Developer, PatientOrderSets.com
Author and Digital Tool Strategist

Accelerate Your Career in Nursing:

A Guide to Professional Advancement and Recognition

Janice Phillips, PhD, RN, FAAN
Janet M. Boivin, BSN, BA, RN

 Sigma Theta Tau International
Honor Society of Nursing

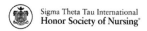
Sigma Theta Tau International
Honor Society of Nursing®

The Honor Society of Nursing, Sigma Theta Tau International (STTI) is a nonprofit organization whose mission is to support the learning, knowledge, and professional development of nurses committed to making a difference in health worldwide. Founded in 1922, STTI is a global community of nurse leaders with 486 chapters in more than 85 countries. Members include practicing nurses, instructors, researchers, policymakers, entrepreneurs, and others. STTI's chapters are located throughout Australia, Botswana, Brazil, Canada, Colombia, Ghana, Hong Kong, Japan, Kenya, Malawi, Mexico, the Netherlands, Pakistan, Portugal, Singapore, South Africa, South Korea, Swaziland, Sweden, Taiwan, Tanzania, United Kingdom, United States, and Wales. More information about STTI can be found online at www.nursingsociety.org.

Sigma Theta Tau International
550 West North Street
Indianapolis, IN, USA 46202

To order additional books, buy in bulk, or order for corporate use, contact Nursing Knowledge International at 888.NKI.4YOU (888.654.4968/US and Canada) or +1.317.634.8171 (outside US and Canada).

To request a review copy for course adoption, email solutions@nursingknowledge.org or call 888.NKI.4YOU (888.654.4968/US and Canada) or +1.317.634.8171 (outside US and Canada).

To request author information, or for speaker or other media requests, contact the Honor Society of Nursing, Sigma Theta Tau International's Marketing Communications group at 888.634.7575 (US and Canada) or +1.317.634.8171 (outside US and Canada).

ISBN: 9781937554583
EPUB ISBN: 9781937554590
PDF ISBN: 9781937554606
MOBI ISBN: 9781937554613

Library of Congress Cataloging-in-Publication Data
Phillips, Janice Mitchell.
  Accelerate your career in nursing : a guide to professional advancement and recognition / Janice Phillips, Janet Boivin.
       p. ; cm.
  Includes bibliographical references.
  ISBN 978-1-937554-58-3 (alk. paper) – ISBN 978-1-937554-59-0 (EPUB) – ISBN 978-1-937554-60-6 (PDF) – ISBN 978-1-937554-61-3 (MOBI)
  I. Boivin, Janet. II. Title.
  [DNLM: 1. Career Mobility. 2. Nursing. 3. Communication. 4. Professional Competence. 5. Staff Development–methods. 6. Vocational Guidance. WY 16]
  RT82
  610.7306'9–dc23
                                        2013013736

First Printing, 2013

Publisher: Renee Wilmeth
Acquisitions Editor: Emily Hatch
Editorial Coordinator: Paula Jeffers
Cover Designer: Michael Tanamachi
Interior Design/Page Layout: Aleata Halbig

Principal Book Editor: Carla Hall
Development and Project Editor: Deb Buehler
Copy Editor: Catherine Schwenk
Proofreader: Erin Geile
Indexer: Jane Palmer

Dedication

This book is dedicated to all of my college professors, colleagues, role models, mentors, and friends who have inspired me to achieve my professional best. I'd also like to make a special dedication to Irma Lee Johnson, my first role model in nursing, for her ongoing love and support over more than three decades of nursing.

–Janice Phillips

Acknowledgments

My sincere thanks to Janet Boivin for her inspiring ideas and diligent editorial assistance, and for being such a joy to work with during this project.

My deepest thanks to a stellar and accomplished team of contributors who shared their time and expertise to make this book a valued and timely resource.

Thanks to Sigma Theta Tau International, the editorial and book acquisitions staff, and especially Emily Hatch, Deb Buehler, and Carla Hall for the opportunity to publish *Accelerate Your Career in Nursing: A Guide to Professional Advancement and Recognition.*

My appreciation to my beloved profession, nursing, the gift that inspires and sustains me on a variety of levels. To God be the Glory.

–Janice Phillips

I want to thank my coauthor and colleague, Janice Phillips, whom I have long admired, for giving me the opportunity to work with her on this book. *Accelerate Your Career in Nursing: A Guide to Professional Advancement and Recognition* was her brainchild and was guided by her vision of how the book could help registered nurses achieve their professional best.

I also want to thank our chapter contributors, some of the profession's best and most effective nursing leaders, for their graciousness in accepting our suggestions and edits for their individual chapters.

I was also grateful to work once again with former colleagues from Sigma Theta Tau International and to Emily Hatch for her assistance along our path to the book's final publication.

–Janet M. Boivin

About the Authors

Janice Phillips, PhD, RN, FAAN

Janice Phillips is an experienced clinician, researcher, educator, and public policy advocate in the health care arena who completed service as a Robert Wood Johnson Foundation Health Policy Fellow (2010-2011), working in the office of Sen. John D. Rockefeller IV (D-WV). With specialties spanning oncology, public health, women's health, health care disparities, and research administration, she has a passion for educating professional and lay audiences on a number of topics, including professional development, health disparities, health advocacy, and breast cancer. Phillips is the recipient of numerous awards and honors, including the 2006 Martin Luther King, Jr. Humanitarian Award from the University of Chicago Medical Center as well as the Distinguished Nurse Alumni Award from the University of Illinois College of Nursing and St. Xavier University. In 2007, she received the Nursing Spectrum Nursing Excellence Award for Advancing and Leading the Profession and, in 2012, she was inducted into the National Black Nurses Association's Institute of Excellence and the Institute of Medicine of Chicago. The author of more than 70 publications and two edited textbooks, Phillips holds a BSN from North Park College, an MS in community health from St. Xavier College, and a PhD from the University of Illinois College of Nursing. She is a member of numerous professional organizations, including the American Public Health Association, American Nurses Association, American Academy of Nursing, National Black Nurses Association, Oncology Nursing Society, and Sigma Theta Tau International. Phillips is an associate professor at Rush University College of Nursing, Chicago, Illinois.

Janet M. Boivin, BSN, BA, RN

Janet M. Boivin has more than 30 years of experience as a nurse journalist and has written for several general and military newspapers. She has a bachelor of science degree in nursing from the University of Southern Maine in Portland, and a bachelor of art degree in journalism from Northeastern University in Boston. She worked as the national editor and writer for Nurse.com (formerly Nursing Spectrum/Nurse Week) for 18 years. She is the only nurse journalist to have traveled to a war zone to write about military nurses caring for the wounded. She traveled to Iraq three times and is one of few journalists to have observed and talked to detainees at Guantanamo Bay Detention Camp in Cuba. She has won several awards for her writing. Boivin served as Sigma Theta Tau International's book acquisitions editor from 2010 to 2011. In December 2011, she finished a 4-month nurse refresher course after 25 years away from the bedside. She now works as a staff nurse in a charitable clinic, where she sees the physical and psychological hardships incurred by some of the nearly 50 million people who cannot afford health care insurance in the United States. She also continues to work as a freelance health care writer.

Contributing Authors

Katherine M. Arroyo, MSN, PCNS-BC, CCRN, is an instructor in Women, Children, and Family Nursing at Rush University in Chicago and counselor for the Gamma Phi Chapter of Sigma Theta Tau International. She received her bachelor of science and master of science in nursing degrees from Valparaiso University in Indiana. She has clinical experience as both a staff nurse and clinical nurse specialist in pediatric critical care with a special interest in congenital heart disease. Through her work in both clinical and academic settings, Arroyo has been actively involved in mentoring, supporting, and evaluating nurses at all levels of practice.

Cynthia Barginere, DNP, RN, FACHE, is vice president for clinical nursing and chief nursing officer at Rush University Medical Center and associate dean for nursing practice at Rush College of Nursing in Chicago, Illinois. Prior to coming to Rush, she served as chief operating officer and chief nursing officer at Baptist Medical Center South, Montgomery, Alabama. Barginere received her undergraduate and graduate degree from the University of Alabama and her doctorate in nursing practice at Samford University in Birmingham, Alabama. She has completed the Johnson & Johnson Wharton Nurse Executive Fellowship and the Robert Wood Johnson Executive Nurse Fellowship. Barginere also served as president of the Alabama Organization of Nurse Leaders.

Anne E. Belcher, PhD, RN, AOCN, FAAN, ANEF, is associate professor and director for the Office for Teaching Excellence at Johns Hopkins University School of Nursing. She has more than 40 years of experience in nursing education, having taught at the baccalaureate, master's, and doctoral levels.

She has held numerous administrative and educator positions throughout her career. Belcher's area of expertise is oncology nursing, and her research interest is psychosocial aspects of cancer with a focus on spiritual care. She holds a bachelor of science in nursing from the University of North Carolina, a master of nursing degree from the University of Washington, and a PhD from Florida State University. She is an advanced oncology certified nurse, a fellow in the American Academy of Nursing, and a fellow in the Academy of Nursing Education. In 2009, Belcher received the National League for Nursing's Excellence in Teaching Award.

Linda Burnes Bolton, DrPH, RN, FAAN, is vice president and chief nursing officer of Cedars-Sinai Health System and is listed among its Top 25 Women in Healthcare. She has recognized expertise in policy, research, performance improvement, and diversity. Burnes Bolton holds a BSN from Arizona State University in Tempe, and an MSN, an MPH and a DrPH from the University of California, Los Angeles. She is past president of the American Academy of Nursing and the National Black Nurses Association. Burnes Bolton has provided leadership at state and national levels for nursing and health services, and she serves as a trustee of the Robert Wood Johnson Foundation and Case Western Reserve University. She also serves on multiple committees and editorial boards.

Susan A. Clark, RN, launched her own lobbying/consulting business, Capital Edge Consulting, LLC, in 2013. She is Illinois' state nurse lobbyist and formerly served as the Illinois Nursing Association's lobbyist and consultant. She has also worked as a contractual consultant and vice president for Consulting4biz, a Springfield, Illinois, company offering an array of lobbying, political action, and association management services. Clark holds a diploma in nursing from Iowa Methodist School of Nursing in Des Moines, Iowa, and has completed coursework in health policy administration at the University of Illinois, Springfield.

Mary J. Connaughton, MS, RN, is the principal/owner of Connaughton Consulting, founded in 1997. She received a BSN from the University of Michigan and a master in nursing administration degree from Boston University. After 5 years as nurse manager at Beth Israel Deaconess Medical Center, she became nursing director at Mount Auburn Hospital and later served 9 years as associate chief nurse at Massachusetts General Hospital. Connaughton has more than 30 years of nursing leadership and health care consulting experience, specializing in resiliency coaching, leadership development, and strategic planning. She has coached scores of health care leaders, individually and in teams, both in practice and academia. Connaughton's leadership programs are designed to help individuals and teams optimize their inherent talents in pursuit of their goals. She is a frequent speaker on leadership topics and author of articles and book chapters on leadership.

Melanie Dreher, PhD, RN, FAAN, is dean of nursing at Rush University in Chicago, Illinois, with previous deanships at University of Miami, University of Massachusetts, and University of Iowa. She was president of the Honor Society of Nursing, Sigma Theta Tau International (STTI), and the Council on Nursing and Anthropology. She received the Brunson Award for Outstanding Achievement for the Advancement of University Women, the Chancellor's Medal from the University of Massachusetts, and a citation from the U.S. ambassador for her contribution to the welfare of Jamaican people. In addition, STTI presents the Melanie C. Dreher Outstanding Dean Award to deans who have made a significant contribution to scholarship and leadership. She serves on the board of directors for Trinity Health Systems, Wellmark, Inc., and the Chicago Board of Health.

Karen Grigsby, PhD, RN, earned a BSN from the University of Cincinnati, a master in nursing degree from the University of Colorado, and a PhD in nursing from the University of Texas at Austin. She is an associate professor, chair of the Families & Health Systems Department, and interim associate dean of academic programs at the University of Nebraska Medical Center in Omaha. She has expertise in leadership, administration, management, and consultation. Her service has focused on various positions within Sigma Theta Tau International at local, regional, and international levels. Grigsby has conducted research in the areas of coaching for academic success, changes in nursing practice with implementation of electronic documentation systems, and ways nurses develop and integrate knowledge into their practice.

Barbara Kitzes Hinch, DNP, ACNP-BC, is an assistant professor in the Department of Adult Health and Gerontological Nursing at Rush University College of Nursing. She holds a BSN from Indiana University in Bloomington and an MSN, a post-master's certificate as an acute care NP, and a DNP from Rush University in Chicago. She has acted as the specialty coordinator of the Adult Acute Care Nurse Practitioner and Critical Care Clinical Nurse Specialist programs since 2006. Hinch has extensive experience guiding graduate students into choosing the best program to match their career goals.

Currently, she practices as an ACNP in the Cardiac Intensive Care Unit at Rush University Medical Center.

Jane Marie Kirschling, PhD, RN, FAAN, is dean of the University of Maryland School of Nursing and university director of interprofessional education at the University of Maryland, Baltimore. Her clinical expertise is in mental health nursing with a focus on end-of-life care. For more than a decade, her scholarship has focused on workforce development with a special emphasis on rural states. At the national level, she began a 2-year term as president of the American Association of Colleges of Nursing in 2012. Kirschling founded the Kentucky Nursing Capacity Consortium and co-convened Kentucky's Action Coalition, which is working to implement the Institute of Medicine's 2010 recommendations in *The Future of Nursing: Leading Change, Advancing Health*. She received her BSN from Viterbo College in La Crosse, Wisconsin, and her MSN and PhD from Indiana University School of Nursing in Bloomington. She is an alumna of the Robert Wood Johnson Foundation Nurse Executive Fellows Program (2000–2003) and is a fellow in the American Academy of Nursing.

Minna B. Masor, MSN, EdD, RN, CCRN, has more than 15 years of nursing experience, primarily in the acute care setting. She holds a BSN from Rush University in Chicago and an MSN from the University of Phoenix. Masor has always had a passion for teaching, and she completed her master in nursing degree with an emphasis in education. She uses her own experiences, as well as her education and clinical expertise, to help nurses from novice to expert level capitalize on their talents and excel along their own journey in health care and beyond. Masor has provided workshops and one-to-one coaching on reésumé writing and portfolio development for both seasoned professional nurses and nursing students. She is a neurosciences clinical coordinator in Chicago, Illinois.

Marcia Murphy, DNP, ANP, FAHA, is an assistant professor in the Department of Adult Health and Gerontological Nursing at Rush University College of Nursing. She holds a BSN from Loyola University, Chicago, and an MSN, a post-master's certificate ANP, and a DNP from Rush University, Chicago. She has served as a specialty coordinator of the adult-gerontology programs since 2006. In this capacity, she is responsible for oversight of the admissions process to the adult-gerontology programs. Murphy has also practiced as an advanced practice nurse for more than 20 years.

Barbara Nichols, DHL, MS, RN, FAAN, is retired CEO of CGFNS International (Commission on Graduates of Foreign Nursing Schools), an international nonprofit organization recognized for its expertise in credential assessment of foreign-educated health professionals. She is president of Barbara Nichols Consultants, a consultancy devoted to leadership development, especially for minority women. Her personal story about leadership is drawn from her national and global experiences in public and private institutions, and the lessons she learned highlight the dynamics of leadership. Nichols holds a diploma from Massachusetts Memorial Hospital School of Nursing, Boston; a baccalaureate in nursing from Case Western Reserve University, Cleveland; and a master of science in behavioral disabilities from the University of Wisconsin-Madison. She is also the recipient of five honorary doctoral degrees for her scholarly work.

Nancy Ridenour, PhD, APRN, BC, FAAN, is dean and professor of the University of New Mexico College of Nursing, where she also chairs the Health Policy Council for the UNM Health Sciences Center. Ridenour holds a BSN, an ANP, an MS, and an FNP from the University of Colorado School of Nursing, Denver. Her PhD is from Texas Tech University, Lubbock. She was a Robert Wood Johnson Health Policy Fellow with the Committee on Ways and Means in the U.S. House of Representatives. Ridenour is a certified family nurse practitioner and successfully mentors faculty and students in obtaining internships, fellowships, and academic promotions. The author of numerous journal articles and contributions to books, she has focused her career on health policy and improving primary health care for underserved populations.

Barbara Swanson, PhD, RN, FAAN, is professor in the Department of Adult Health & Gerontological Nursing and director of the PhD program in nursing science at Rush University. She holds a BSN from Elmhurst College in Illinois; an MSN from Loyola University, Chicago; and a PhD from Rush University, Chicago. She conducts research to test the effects of marine oils to favorably modulate parameters of inflammation and immune senescence in persons with HIV/AIDS. Swanson has published more than 80 articles and book chapters and serves on several journal editorial boards.

Antonia M. Villarruel, PhD, FAAN, is professor and the Nola J. Pender Collegiate Chair at the University of Michigan. Villarruel holds a BSN from Nazareth College in Kalamazoo, Michigan; an MSN from the University of Pennsylvania in Philadelphia; and a PhD from Wayne State University in Detroit, as well as a postdoctoral fellowship from the University of Michigan in Ann Arbor. She has extensive research and practice in health promotion and health disparities. She incorporates a community-engaged approach to her research, and her most notable work focuses on developing and testing interventions to reduce sexual risk behavior among Mexican and Latino youth. Her NIH-funded program, Cuídate!, has been disseminated nationally by the CDC and other government agencies. She has assumed leadership roles in many national and local organizations. She is a member of the Institute of Medicine and a fellow in the American Academy of Nursing.

Debra Werner, MLIS, is librarian for science instruction and outreach and biomedical reference librarian at the University of Chicago's John Crerar Library. In these roles, she coordinates instruction services for the sciences and provides instruction to members of the university's biomedical community, including students, faculty, clinicians, and researchers. As the library's selector for nursing, she works closely with the Department of Nursing to acquire materials that meet its clinical, educational, and research needs; she also meets regularly with nurses to assist in locating information for their research or practice. She is a member of the University of Chicago Medicine's Nursing Research Committee. Werner has a BA in biology from Augustana College in Rock Island, Illinois, and she received her MLIS from Dominican University in River Forest, Illinois.

Benson Wright, MSN, RN, is the Magnet program coordinator at Rush University Medical Center. He received his BSN from Nell Hodgson Woodruff School of Nursing at Emory University in 2005 and his MSN from Rush University College of Nursing in 2012. Wright served as president of Rush University Medical Center's professional nursing staff from 2011–2013. He is an active member of Sigma Theta Tau International, serving on the International Service Learning Taskforce and the board of Gamma Phi, the Rush College of Nursing chapter. He also chairs the Nursing Care Committee Consortium of the Illinois Organization of Nurse Leaders (IONL).

Susan Wysocki, WHNP, FAANP, holds an associate's degree in nursing from Lasell Junior College in Auburndale, Massachusetts; a bachelor of science in nursing from Boston College in Newton, Massachusetts; and a certificate as a women's health NP from Planned Parenthood Federation of America and the New Jersey College of Medicine. She became a nurse practitioner in 1975 and was a pioneer in advancing the role. Wysocki chaired the National Alliance for Nurse Practitioners from 1990 to 1991, and in 1993, she was one of five NPs to organize a meeting of state and national NP organizations that formed the National Nurse Practitioner Coalition. That organization later became the American College of Nurse Practitioners, where she served as founding president from 1994 to 1995. Her awards and recognition include the Miriam Manisoff award for advancing WHNPs, the Who's Who in the NP Movement award (*The Nurse Practitioner* journal), the lifetime achievement award at the National Conference for Nurse Practitioners, a charter fellowship in the American Academy of Nurse Practitioners, and ACNP's Sharp Cutting Edge Award.

Table of Contents

Foreword: A GPS for Gaining More Health Care Influence xix

Introduction xxi

Chapter 1: First Lessons: Know Yourself and Your Values 1
Foundational Elements for a Successful Career 2
Personal Values: The Foundation of Your Career 2
Knowledge and Skills: A Constantly Expanding Continuum 5
Effective Communication Requires Honest Self-Appraisal 6
Capitalizing on Your Strengths and Identifying Opportunities for Growth. . . 8
Recognize and Acknowledge the Strengths That Others Bring to
the Workplace 10
Know Your Areas for Personal and Professional Growth 10
What Is Your Preferred Future? 12
Build Your Plan 13
Build Your Model of Sufficiency 15
Self-Knowledge/Self-Awareness 16

Chapter 2: Nursing Organizations 2.0. 21
Advantages of Joining a Professional Organization. 22
Matching Your Goals With the Right Professional Organization 23
Benefits of Organizations. 23
Join a Professional Organization. 26
Keeping Your Resume Current. 27

Chapter 3: Let Your Light Shine: Portfolio Principles. 29
The Value of a Portfolio. 30
What Is a Nursing Portfolio? 32
The Advanced Portfolio 36
The Electronic Portfolio 39
Portfolio Designs 39
When to Use a Nursing Portfolio 40
Advantages of the Nursing Portfolio 41
Ready, Set, Go Create Your Portfolio 41

Chapter 4: Cultivating Recognition. 45
Why Professional Recognition for RNs Is Necessary and Appropriate 46
Developing Plans for Professional Recognition 47
Creating Your Vision 48
Conducting a Self-Assessment 48
Developing a Plan 50
Developing a Successful Nomination 51
Identifying the Right Award. 53
Determining the Right Time to Submit a Nomination. 53
Identifying the Right Nominators. 54
Writing and Submitting a Successful Application. 54

Chapter 5: Igniting Your Cheering Section 57
Recommendation Formats 58
  "Bank" Your Recommenders 61
  Understand the Application. 65
  Choosing the Right Recommenders. 65
  Applicant Responsibilities 68
  Handling Awkward Situations 73
  Social Media Recommendations 75
Your Ready to Go 76

Chapter 6: Graduate School: Crafting Successful Applications . . . 79
Mapping a Strategy for the Application Process. 80
Four to Six Months Prior to Application Deadline. 82
  The Application Form. 82
  The Resume 82
  Graduate Record Exam 83
  Academic Transcripts 83
Less than Four Months Prior to Application Deadline 83
  Letters of Recommendation. 83
  Provide Essential Details 85
  The Essay 85
  Singularity. 86
  Tailored 86
  Organized. 86
  Professional. 87
One Month Prior to Application Deadline 89
  The Interview Process 90
  Preparing for the Interview 91
  Questions to Expect from MSN and DNP Program Interviewers. 91
  Questions to Expect from PhD Program Interviewers 91
  Questions to Ask MSN and DNP Program Interviewers 92
  Questions to Ask PhD Program Interviewers 92
The Interview 92
Last Step in the Process 93
Conclusion 94

Chapter 7: Landing Fellowships and Internships 97
Internships and Fellowships Help You Shine 98
Internships and Fellowships 99
What Will You Gain? 101
Pursuing Opportunities. 103
Winning Strategies for Success 104
Preparing for the Interview. 106
  What Can You Expect After the Interview?. 108
  What to Do if You Are Not Selected 108
  Congratulations! You've Been Accepted 108
  Resources for Internships 109

Resources for Fellowships 110
Nontraditional Resources for Fellowships and Internships. 111

Chapter 8: Expressing Your Professional Best 113
Persuasive Communication Requires Planning, Understanding, and
Self-Awareness. 114
Good Listening Skills Cannot Be Overemphasized. 116
Theories of Persuasion 117
Nonverbal Communication. 122
Social Networking 123
Appreciative Inquiry. 124
Persuasive Presentations to Groups 125

Chapter 9: Advocating for the Nursing Profession. 129
Be Prepared. 131
Illustrate the Problem With More Than Facts. 131
Make No Assumptions About Your Audience 133
Be a Resource. 133
Disruptive Innovations 134
Working With Organizations: Think Outside the Box. 136
Participating in Nursing Organizations 137
Final Thoughts 138

Chapter 10: How to Act Powerfully 139
Act Like You Mean It. 140
Introduce Yourself With Pride. 141
Be Empowered at the Bedside 143
Gain Power Through Advocacy, Political Activism, and Politics. 145

Chapter 11: Two of Nursing's Finest: Their Personal Journeys. . 147
Expressing Your Best as a Leader: Initial Steps on the Journey 148
Learning to Lead in the Community. 149
Learning to Lead in Your Profession: Strategies for Professional
Advancement 151
Volunteer Leadership Experiences 151
My Experience With the Department of Veterans Affairs. 154
Leading in Society: Creating a Virtual Leadership Community 155
Nursing Leadership 156
Leadership Organizations. 156
Public Sector Volunteer Leadership 157
Foundations 158
The Dynamics of Leadership: A Personal Perspective 159
Concluding Thoughts. 164

Appendix: Resources for Success 165
Tools to Keep Current: So Much Information, So Little Time 165
RSS. 166
Alerts 167
Social Media. 168

What to Read?... 168
  Type of Article 169
  Deciding Which Journals to Invest Your Time With 170
  Read Like a Pro 171
  Keeping Track of What You've Read 172
  Continuing Education 175
  Journals and eJournals..................................... 176
  Databases 177
  Professional Organizations and Associations.................... 177
  Commercial Websites 177
  Conferences 178
  Institutional Initiatives..................................... 178

Index 179

Foreword

A GPS for Gaining More Health Care Influence

Our country desperately needs to prepare the next generation of nurses to meet the clinical, financial, technological, and ethical challenges facing our 21st-century health care system. As the Affordable Care Act is fully implemented in the next several years, nurses must be well positioned if they are to reach the echelons of power where they can help shape the new health care landscape.

True, nurses are no longer shut out of boardrooms, C-suites, research facilities, or state or national capitals, where the decisions that affect our patients are made. Yet they are not entirely welcome, either. There are not enough registered nurses at policy- and decision-making tables to influence the debate on how to improve patient care.

In a recent Gallup poll, 1,500 health opinion leaders said they wanted nurses to have more influence in a variety of areas, especially in reducing medical errors, increasing quality of care, and promoting wellness. They also believed that nurses should have more input and impact in planning, policy development, and management (Khoury, Blizzard, Moore, & Hassmiller, 2011).

But to do this, nurses need to know where their careers are headed and how to get there. They need to recognize and document their accomplishments to put themselves in the right places at the right times—when policymakers are selected to help shape health care policy.

Accelerate Your Career in Nursing: A Guide to Professional Advancement and Recognition is a GPS for nurses who want to navigate beyond the traditional boundaries of the profession and become involved in making truly influential health care decisions. This book is also in sync with two major goals of The Future of Nursing: Campaign for Action, a joint initiative of the Robert Wood Johnson Foundation and AARP: increasing nursing leadership and promoting nursing education.

The campaign is working to prepare nurses to address our nation's most pressing health care challenges—access, quality, and cost—by helping to implement the evidence-based recommendations from *The Future of Nursing: Leading Change, Advancing Health*, a report from the Institute of Medicine (2011). More information about the campaign is available at www.campaignforaction.org.

Our nation faces pressing health care challenges, including an aging and more diverse population, more patients with chronic conditions, millions more who are uninsured, soaring costs, and a shortage of providers. We can address these challenges now by maximizing the use of nurses. *Accelerate Your Career in Nursing: A Guide to Professional Advancement and Recognition* will help you maximize your unique skills, education, and experiences.

Compiled and edited by Janice Phillips and Janet M. Boivin, this book provides you with the necessary information and instruction to recognize and document your accomplishments so you can advance your career. This practical and readily accessible resource provides valuable insight on everything from crafting successful graduate school applications to developing your portfolio to advocating for professional nursing organizations and associations.

It is my hope that aspiring nurse leaders, educators, policymakers, and clinicians will read this book and follow the wisdom and expertise laid out by some of our country's most accomplished nursing leaders. I firmly believe that this book will help you lead system change and improve patient care.

–*Susan B. Hassmiller, PhD, RN, FAAN*
RWJF Senior Adviser for Nursing and Director,
Future of Nursing: Campaign for Action

References

American Hospital Association. *AHA hospital statistics* (2011 ed.). Chicago, IL: Author.

The Institute of Medicine. (2011). *The future of nursing: Leading change, advancing health*. Washington, DC: The National Academies Press (prepublication copy). Retrieved from http://www.nap.edu/catalog/12956.html

Khoury, C. M., Blizzard, R., Moore, L. W., & Hassmiller, S. (2011). Nursing leadership from bedside to boardroom: A Gallup national survey of opinion leaders. *Journal of Nursing Administration, 41*(7/8), 299–305.

Introduction

Welcome to *Accelerate Your Career in Nursing: A Guide to Professional Advancement and Recognition.*

This text was inspired, in part, by the Affordable Care Act and the Institute of Medicine's (IOM) and Robert Wood Johnson Foundation's *Future of Nursing* reports, both of which call for transformation of the nursing profession through advanced education, expansion of leadership, and practice of nursing at higher levels. These and other reports underscore the need for nurses to develop the necessary skills, education, sophistication, and confidence that will gain them a seat at the various tables where health care decisions and policies are formed, whether within for-profit or nonprofit health care organizations or state and local governments.

Too often, frontline nurses in hospitals, clinics, outpatient centers, hospice, and home health care do not think of themselves as leaders or recognize their own contributions. If they cannot do so, how can they be expected to leverage their accomplishments to benefit patients, health care, or their own careers? Yet the Affordable Care Act and the *Future of Nursing* reports call for just such nursing expertise and knowledge.

Accelerate Your Career in Nursing: A Guide to Professional Advancement and Recognition spells out how nurses can recognize and document their accomplishments and then use them to advance within health care. Our ultimate goal is that this book will, in turn, give nurses the credentials they need to earn a place at the health care table, in whatever setting that may be.

Within the book's chapters, a cadre of nurse leaders in education, academia, research, health care administration, and health policy share expertise and wisdom. Each author or author team discusses a number of current and emerging topics to help complement the various stages of your career trajectory. A complementary feature of this book is that the authors recount a defining personal moment in their professional careers and its connection to their respective chapters.

The content and special features of this book reflect the increased need for nurses to express their professional best and validate their distinction of excellence in today's health care arena. Each chapter provides helpful tips, informative tables, and resources and examples needed to advance professionally. In addition, we include personal stories based on the experiences of each author. These pieces, titled "In Real Life," reflect the author's vast expertise and passion for the nursing profession. "Remember This" sections highlight major themes in each chapter, while those titled "Good to Know" offer relevant information for your consideration.

Chapters 1–4: Developing and Identifying Your Distinction of Excellence will introduce you to a number of self-assessment tools, resources, and inventories designed to help you identify and leverage your strengths in the workplace, develop high-quality nursing portfolios, and select organizations that will facilitate your professional development and contributions in health care.

Part I is designed to encourage self-reflection on your career path as you set forth to identify and document your contributions to health care and the nursing profession. The authors offer essential advice on how to accurately assess and document your personal distinction of excellence, an essential skill that will create a leading edge when seeking professional recognition and advancement.

Chapters 5–7: Putting Your Best Foot Forward explores strategies and tools for expressing your best when seeking selection for competitive graduate programs, fellowships, or internships. Authors of this section provide timely, firsthand insights on how to achieve success by putting your best foot forward when crafting competitive applications. Readers are encouraged to strategically select nominators and sponsors, thereby avoiding the "ask anybody" approach to securing letters of recommendation. Part II is designed to help you secure and compile the necessary evidence to distinguish and validate your distinction of excellence.

Chapters 8–10: Expressing Your Best for the Profession will help you on your path to persuasive communication. Here you will gain insights on how to speak and present yourself so that others will take notice. From the bedside to the boardroom, persuasive communication is an imperative tool for advancing your career and securing recognition. Authors share insights on how to use persuasive communication to advance professionally or advocate on behalf of the profession.

Chapter 11: Experts Lead the Charge describes the unique paths of two distinguished nurse leaders who have helped to advance the nursing profession. Both have served in highly visible and influential positions throughout their careers. Read inspiring stories in which they share what they learned and accomplished during their journey to progressive leadership in nursing and health care. Finally, the nurse leaders share personal insights into the process of contributing to the nursing profession.

Whether you're a novice or an expert nurse, we hope that you and future generations will be inspired to reach your highest level of professional advancement, recognition, and satisfaction in nursing. You will find *Accelerate Your Career in Nursing: A Guide to Professional Advancement and Recognition* a valuable and trusted resource throughout your professional career.

"YOU GAIN STRENGTH, COURAGE AND CONFIDENCE BY EVERY EXPERIENCE IN WHICH YOU REALLY STOP TO LOOK FEAR IN THE FACE. YOU MUST DO THE THING YOU THINK YOU CANNOT DO."

–ELEANOR ROOSEVELT

Chapter 1

First Lessons: Know Yourself and Your Values

–Jane Marie Kirschling and Mary J. Connaughton

AFTER READING THIS CHAPTER, YOU WILL BE ABLE TO:

- Understand the role that personal values, acquired knowledge and skills, and effective communication have on career success

- Identify ways to leverage strengths and pinpoint areas for improvement to achieve optimum career growth

- Understand the importance of creating a self-reflective practice to assure alignment of goals with career choices

- Describe how building your model of sufficiency promotes self-responsibility, bolsters self-confidence, and supports individuals on their journey to be their best

No two nurses follow the same exact path in their nursing careers. This results in a richness of experiences that directly impacts how you individually and collectively approach your "work"—whether in direct patient care, caring for communities, serving in a nursing leadership role, educating the next generation of nurses, generating new knowledge for the discipline and health care, and/or engaging in service to your communities or profession. Irrespective of where you are in your nursing career, there are always opportunities to grow.

Foundational Elements for a Successful Career

So where to begin? It is important to consider the foundational elements for shaping your career, recognizing that these elements will evolve over time as we individually and collectively turn the kaleidoscope to reshape health care in the United States and globally. Key elements at this point in time include personal values, knowledge and skills, and effective communication.

Personal Values: The Foundation of Your Career

Personal values guide how you enact the work of nursing over time. Whether a recent graduate or someone with more than 20 years of experience, you must take time to consider and articulate your personal values. Seeing how your core values are reflected in the actual work of nursing allows you to optimize your contributions through patient-centered care as a registered nurse or an advanced practice registered nurse, generate new knowledge for the discipline as a nurse scientist, prepare the next generation of nurses as a faculty member, or design the delivery of health care as a nurse leader.

What are your core values? Write down your core values and revisit the list from time to time, reflecting on points of tension and any potential link to your work. Although there are hundreds of values that you could identify, hone your list to three to five key values, focusing on those that truly shape how you engage with others on a daily basis.

One strategy for reflection is to list your values on a small note card and carry this in your purse or wallet. This increases the likelihood that you will look over the list from time to time, reflecting on it as a barometer for how fully you are able to live your core values, both in your personal and professional life. The authors' core values statements, as well as those of two other nurses, are provided for your consideration below.

CORE VALUE STATEMENTS

Mary J. Connaughton

Mary J. Connaughton graduated with a BSN from the University of Michigan in 1972. Her early job choices were based on geography (ocean, then mountains). She quickly learned that there is a direct correlation between the quality of the practice environment and the effectiveness of nursing leadership. She expected that the high value she placed on patient-centered care *and a* collegial, supportive work environment *would be the norm, but this was not reality. She was in so much professional distress about not being able to practice according to her values that she nearly left the profession. Her father gave her wise advice...to become the leader she was seeking in others. Despite the admonition of some colleagues that she was going over to the dark side, Mary completed her master's degree in nursing administration and went on to hold nurse manager and then nursing director positions for 18 years. She was fortunate to find wonderful role models and* mentors, Joyce Clifford, Trish Gibbons, and Yvonne Munn, *who helped to shape her leadership identity. A* passion for leadership *fueled her practice, knowing that leadership excellence is essential to ensure that patients and families receive competent, customized, compassionate care. Mary's commitment to* developing others *through mentoring and coaching led her to start a consulting business in 1997 that focused on resiliency coaching and leadership development. True to her core values, her mission is to support health care leaders in practice and academia to be at their best.*

Penne Allison

Penne Allison completed her bachelor of science in nursing in 1983. She initially began her career in a 6-month pediatric nurse intern program. Penne completed a master of science in operation management in 1993 and has served in various capacities within emergency services, including staff nurse, clinical nurse educator,

continues

continued

trauma coordinator, and director. Penne is currently a director at an inner-city emergency department (ED)/level 1 trauma center and a community ED. Her first core value is to be a lifelong learner. *She is an avid reader and believes nurses should always keep up with the latest evidence to achieve optimal patient outcomes. Secondly, she values* teamwork. *The ED is an area where teamwork is necessary, or patients could suffer. Teamwork should encompass every caregiver who interacts with the patient. Proper communication and hand-offs make the team function properly. Thirdly, Penne values* leadership. *Everything rises and falls on leadership. Leaders create the patient care environment, which starts at the bedside with the staff nurse. Every nurse has the responsibility to take initiative and to be an advocate for his or her patient. Lastly, Penne values* people. *Valuing people starts with the patient and the family. Being patient-centered is why nursing exists; nurses help patients to see the important role they play in their own healing. Not only is the patient/family valuable, but the nurse is as well. Serving as a coach at various stages of Penne's career has given her the opportunity to encourage leadership, scholarship, and coalition building within and outside of nursing.*

Karen Hill

Karen Hill completed her associate degree in nursing in 1978. One core value evident early in her career was her value of education. *Karen realized as a staff nurse in the operating room that although she did not know what direction her career would take, it would be necessary to advance her education to be ready for the challenges that lay ahead. Karen went on to complete her BSN, MSN, and DNP degrees. Another guiding core value for Karen is to* treat patients as you would want your family treated. *Karen exemplified this value by the way she treated her own bedside patients as well as in her role as chief operating officer/chief nursing officer, where she works with nurses and other care providers. One last value Karen upholds is to* appreciate the opportunities that others have afforded her in her career *and to* offer mentoring and coaching *to others as they advance their careers and competencies. Karen develops and offers transition-to-practice programs for new nurses as well as transition-to-leadership opportunities for experienced staff.*

Jane Kirschling

Jane Kirschling completed her baccalaureate degree in nursing in 1980 and immediately headed to graduate school, where she completed her MSN in 1982 and her PhD in 1984. Jane's parents were unwavering in their commitment that their three children would pursue higher education, *a value that remains core to her career. (She has spent nearly 30 years as a university faculty member and administrator.) Jane's oldest brother was instrumental in encouraging her to pursue her graduate degrees early in her nursing career, which has served her well over time. Although she occasionally met resistance from other nurses who argued that she had limited hands-on nursing experience, she has had two exceptional mentors, Angela Barron McBride and Patricia Archbold, who have offered her sage advice throughout her career. Another of her core value focuses on* hard work, *always being willing to roll up her sleeves to help accomplish the goal at hand. You cannot minimize the message you send to your coworkers when you offer to help. Two additional values that have guided Jane's career are a* commitment to treat others fairly *and a* desire to remain humble. *Nursing students are continually asked to grow and stretch. Allowing students to create a safe learning environment involves giving students the space to take risks, knowing that in the end, their faculty will be fair in assessing their learning. Whether at the bedside or in the classroom, much of what we accomplish is on the shoulders of others and requires collaboration to get the best possible outcome. At the core of nursing is the ability to use your knowledge and skills to impact the lives of others; effectively communicate with those under your care (often in less than ideal circumstances); and effectively work with other health care providers, recognizing when you do not have the answer and need to rely on someone else to guide your decisions to achieve desired outcomes.*

Knowledge and Skills: A Constantly Expanding Continuum

The knowledge and skills acquired in entry-level nursing programs and advanced practice registered nurse (APRN) programs are only the starting point for novice nurses or APRNs. Practice expertise comes with experience and an unwavering commitment to real-time learning. This professional growth is multipronged. It includes practicing with other providers who willingly share their knowledge and expertise in a nonjudgmental way. Growth is also the result of an unwavering commitment to lifelong learning and curiosity about best practice.

You are responsible for optimizing your knowledge and skills over time and accepting and embracing the fact that at any point in time, you can be at varying points along the novice-to-expert continuum. Within the framework of your current work, it is important to ask:

In the next 3 to 6 months:

- What do you need to learn more about in order to be more effective in your work?

- Are the learning needs you have identified consistent with those identified by your supervisor? If not, how do you align these learning needs to further support your competency?

- What are your available resources?

With answers to these questions in hand, the next step is to lay out a realistic plan for further developing your knowledge and skills and to follow through on that plan.

Effective Communication Requires Honest Self-Appraisal

The ability to effectively communicate is critical to achieving the desired health care outcomes. The American Academy on Communication in Healthcare's tagline captures it well: "Better communication. Better relationships. Better care" (http://www.aachonline.org). It is critical to recognize that interpersonal relationships, often with relative strangers (e.g., other providers, patients, or family caregivers), are at the core of health care delivery.

Although the ability to effectively communicate is influenced by a wide array of factors, such as a high stress environment, language barriers, and fatigue, it is essential to continually strive to improve communication skills in order to achieve the best possible outcomes. At a minimum, communication is a two-way street, with two or more individuals giving and receiving information. Upon realizing that there has been a breakdown in communication, pause and try to learn from the situation. This requires honest appraisal about what could have been done differently to achieve a better outcome and to expand your communication toolkit.

Expanding your communication toolkit, as well as your ability to work effectively in teams, is a major focus of the U.S. Department of Health and Human Services Agency for Healthcare Research and Quality (AHRQ) TeamSTEPPS initiative. TeamSTEPPS is a teamwork system designed for health care professionals that is:

- A powerful solution to improving patient safety within your organization

- An evidence-based teamwork system to improve communication and teamwork skills among health care professionals

- A source for ready-to-use materials and a training curriculum to successfully integrate teamwork principles into all areas of your health care system

- Scientifically rooted in more than 20 years of research and lessons from the application of teamwork principles

Developed by Department of Defense's Patient Safety Program in collaboration with the Agency for Healthcare Research and Quality. (http://teamstepps.ahrq.gov)

This initiative provides a rich resource for nurses and other health care providers. By periodically doing a web search on "health care communication," you will find additional resources that can be added to your communication toolkit, including the following examples.

EXAMPLES OF COMMUNICATION TOOLS:

As noted by the U.S. Department of Health and Human Services Indian Health Service "Ask Me 3" campaign, "clear communication is the foundation for patients to be able to understand and act on health information." (http://www.ihs.gov/healthcommunications/ index.cfm?module=dsp_hc_toolkit)

The U.S. Department of Defense and TriService have designed a tool, "I PASS the BATON," to increase the likelihood that the handoff of a patient from one provider ensures the continuum of patient care. (http://www.unmc.edu/rural/patient-safety/tool-time/TT2-053006-DOD-SBAR-SafetyBriefings/DOD%20Handoff%20-%20I%20 Pass%20the%20Baton.pdf)

Capitalizing on Your Strengths and Identifying Opportunities for Growth

All nurses, irrespective of how long they have practiced, bring individual strengths to the workplace. For example, take the neonatal nurse who has the uncanny ability to work with drug-addicted mothers, calmly guiding a mother to gently touch her baby's tiny arm despite the array of IV tubes.

Or the emergency department nurse who carefully assesses the elderly man who arrived via an ambulance, having fallen at a local nursing home.

Or the nurse manager who welcomes a new graduate onto the unit, ensuring that he or she will have protected time to actively participate in the hospital's post-BSN residency program. It is important that we recognize and acknowledge our strengths. This is easier said than done.

In the nursing culture, individuals are more likely to be aware of personal shortcomings than individual strengths and are more likely to spend time being critical (of themselves and others) than acknowledging the positive attributes and contributions each person brings to work. There is a tendency in the nursing profession to downplay strengths and even to dismiss compliments about talents or skills. It is not arrogant to project and articulate your strengths. It is a sign of good leadership to know yourself, what you and others can rely on, and what you are working on to improve. It is false humility to suggest: "Oh, it was nothing. Anyone in my position would have recognized the patient was going into shock." "I am not so special. I just really like the challenge of dealing with difficult families." "It is not a big deal. I just happen to be a cheerful person, even on the worst days."

A key to building self-confidence is being able to name your strengths—the skills, talents, experiences, or aspects of your character or personality that serve you well regardless of the situation. This does not happen by accident. It involves a purposeful, periodic, inward look at who you are, not comparing yourself to others to see how you measure up. As you grow and change, it is important to stay in touch with who you are becoming. Telling anyone who will listen that "I avoid conflict like the plague" is yesterday's news if you have been working on improving your conflict management skills and now handle most situations successfully. Only regular self-reflection on where you excel and what you are working to improve will keep you current.

Why is this important? Your patients, families, students, and colleagues, indeed, the entire health care system, need every nurse to function at the highest capacity to optimize the positive impact of nursing on the health and well-being of society. If you are hiding your light in the shadows, refusing to acknowledge the tremendous strengths you have to offer, then you will never fully achieve your best practice.

If you excel in a crisis situation by using your ability to stay focused in chaos; if you always see the humanity in other human beings, regardless of their negative emotions; if your excellent organizational skills make you incredibly productive; if your humor never leaves you no matter how sad or stressful the circumstance; if you always tell the truth, regardless of the consequences; if you are always fair and objective; if you treat every single person with respect; if you have the capacity to always see the big picture; if you have a gift to be able to articulate complex ideas with clarity, then let these gifts and talents and skills shine. By knowing your strengths, you will more confidently bring your whole self forward for the greater good.

IN REAL LIFE: MARY CONNAUGHTON

It is not always obvious in the moment that an ordinary conversation will in hindsight be seen as transformative. This was the case when I had my first performance review as associate chief nurse at Massachusetts General Hospital with Yvonne Munn, chief nursing officer. The review was a favorable experience: I received positive feedback about the changes I had led in my division in my first year and guidance about areas of my leadership practice that needed to improve. The meeting couldn't have been better. As I was making a move to leave, Yvonne said, leaning into the table: "Mary, I have just one question for you...where does your lack of self-confidence come from?" Busted! As far as I knew, up to this moment, my insecurities and self-doubt were my little secret. I pondered this question over and over and concluded that there was no reason in the world I should lack confidence. I began to notice how often I had an internal voice diminishing my contributions. This provocative question sent me on a journey to embrace myself for who I am, to take pride in my accomplishments and to see my shortcomings as opportunities to grow. Not only am I living a more authentic life, but I found the courage to start my own consulting business to help other nurse leaders be the best they can be. Thank you, Yvonne Munn, for demonstrating the power of saying what you see. Twenty-five years later, it has made all the difference.

Recognize and Acknowledge the Strengths That Others Bring to the Workplace

This commitment should not be the responsibility of a handful of coworkers or be limited to nurses who hold leadership positions. It is a collective responsibility to create a culture of appreciation of one another's strengths.

Stop and think about the last time you acknowledged a fellow nurse for the outstanding care that he or she provided. You could write a personal handwritten note, publicly thank him or her in a staff meeting, or talk with the supervisor about how helpful he or she was with a particularly difficult family member. And, when you find yourself on the receiving end of a compliment, receive it with grace and do not minimize the situation. Simply accept the appreciation and thank whomever for acknowledging your work. Also reflect on the compliment, because this is a helpful strategy for recognizing your strengths as a professional nurse.

Know Your Areas for Personal and Professional Growth

This work is not for the faint of heart because it requires honest self-reflection and the ability to engage others that you trust to provide constructive feedback. It is not unusual for nurses who return to school to feel out of their normal skin being a student again. You are never too old to learn, so although it is natural to feel like a fish out of water, you have to embrace that desire to always pursue learning opportunities. Key to getting beyond these feelings is recognizing that you never achieve perfection and that you always have opportunities to learn and grow.

Within your employment setting, there are an array of resources that can guide your self-reflection on strengths and areas for improvement, such as tools that measure ongoing skill competencies, annual or biannual performance evaluations, purposefully engaging with your supervisor or peers on an area for professional growth, and actively participating in new graduate orientation or nurse residency programs. It is critical that you do not see this as a one-time opportunity, but rather an ongoing process that becomes a natural part of your nursing practice. The products of your self-reflection should be a part of your nursing portfolio, allowing you the opportunity to go back and review your previous assessments. If you have not done so, we recommend that you connect with your department's nurse educator offices to see what resources are available.

Over the years, we have found various standardized tools to be helpful to individuals and teams when exploring opportunities for individual and collective growth. With the support of a facilitator, completing the tools and then using them to engage in conversation provide an opportunity to learn with and about one another. When doing this work, it is important to acknowledge that there is not one correct profile, but instead a range of ways in which individuals approach one another and the work that they do. A small sampling of tools is provided here for you to further explore this option.

- **Campbell-Hallam Team Leader Profile (TLP)** incorporates an assessment of team leadership skills and practices that is completed by members and observers of your team.

- **DiSC Classic** provides a framework for human behavior including gaining knowledge about an individual's unique behavioral pattern.

- **Emergenetics Profile** assesses how you think and behave so that you can make better decisions, work better in teams, and discover your natural strengths.

- **EQ Map** explores facets that make up personal emotional intelligence in relationship to performance, creativity, and success.

- **Fundamental Interpersonal Relations Orientation-Behavior Assessment (FIRO-B)** depicts how an individual's needs for inclusion, control, and affection can shape his or her interactions with others.

- **Herrmann Brain Dominance Instrument (HBDI)** explains the way an individual prefers to think, learn, communicate, and make decisions.

- **Myers-Briggs Type Indicator (MBTI)** identifies psychological preferences in how you perceive the world and make decisions. Free online inventories that reflect aspects of the MBTI are available. For example, the Jung Typology Test is available at http://www.humanmetrics.com/cgi-win/jtypes2 and The Cognitive Style Inventory is available at http://www.myersbriggs.org.

- **SKILLSCOPE** gathers feedback from a boss, direct reports, and peers on 15 management skills (e.g., informational skills, decisional skills, interpersonal skills, personal resources, and effective use of self).

- **SYMLOG** (System for the Multiple Level Observation of Groups) assesses key factors known to directly influence effectiveness.

What Is Your Preferred Future?

Although it is easy to get caught up in living one day at a time, juggling the multiple responsibilities of family, friends, and work, it is important to reflect on your preferred future. A preferred future is one that you design and take ownership for planning, followed by conscious choices that support your goal. Sometimes your career unfolds almost magically, with seemingly little initiative on your part.

There is always the potential, however, that something bigger than you imagined possible could emerge when you dare to dream about your future and involve others who know you well. On the other hand, there is nothing wrong with being content with the work that you are currently doing.

However, if you aspire to advance your education or increase your level of responsibility at work, then you need to have a plan for accomplishing these goals. Key to advancing your nursing career has been the potential your mentors saw in you, and your ability to trust that whatever the opportunity, you would learn and grow personally and professionally as you assumed additional responsibility.

IN REAL LIFE: JANE KIRSCHLING

A critical turning point in my career occurred in 1994 when Dean Carol Lindeman asked me to assume the role of associate dean for graduate studies at the Oregon Health Sciences University School of Nursing. I had served as a faculty member and had been tenured and promoted to professor. My initial response was to say "no," but instead I asked Dean Lindeman why she felt I was ready to assume this administrative role. She quickly pointed out that I knew the graduate programs within the school, since I had taught master's and PhD students, and that I seemed to enjoy faculty governance work. She felt that my openness to hearing different points of view would serve me well as I worked with others to reach consensus on how best to move various graduate program issues forward. I decided to trust Dean Lindeman's sense that I could do a good job in the associate dean role and now have nearly 20 years of experience in higher education administration.

If you have access to a career counselor at your place of employment, use this resource as a sounding board. If not, engage in conversation with trusted colleagues and/or engage the services of a career coach. Being purposeful when asking yourself the following five questions can help shape your plans for the next 1 to 5 years:

- Are you satisfied with your current work? If not, what needs to happen so that you can more fully engage in your nursing career?

- Are you committed to working for your current employer? If so, what other opportunities exist for you to advance within this organization? What knowledge or skills do you need to obtain to be eligible for advancement? Who within the organization can mentor you to advance your career?

- Do you want to practice as an APRN? If so, how soon do you want to begin graduate school, and do you want to pursue a master in nursing or a doctor of nursing practice (DNP) degree?

- Do you want to impact the future of health through the generation of new knowledge? If so, what BSN to PhD and MSN to PhD programs offer the opportunity to further specialize in your areas of expertise?

- What will you need from your family and friends in order to accomplish your career goals?

Build Your Plan

With answers to these questions in hand, the next step is to lay out a realistic plan. Invite others to review your plan and to provide you with support to accomplish your goals. If for whatever reason the plan does not come together as you initially designed it, do not worry. Revise the plan and reset your course of action. Your commitment to the foundational elements of a successful nursing career and to your personal and professional growth is key.

A theme in this chapter is taking responsibility for your personal growth and future. When this proactive approach is used, it serves to build your confidence and helps strengthen your leadership skills. There is no limit to the sense of pride and joy you gain from experiencing the fruits of high-level engagement, putting values in action, exhibiting efforts to learn and grow, and steering toward a future that is in alignment with your passion and talents.

Periodically revisiting the preceding five questions will allow you to shape the images that appear in the kaleidoscope of your nursing career. It is the richness of the multiple images that appear over time that will define the contributions that you have and will continue to make, knowing that along the way you used your evolving nursing knowledge and skills to make a difference in the lives that you touched.

IN REAL LIFE:

We have found that using a career coach both for ourselves, as well as others who report to us, has allowed us to shape our nursing careers. For example, as dean of a college of nursing, Jane Kirschling had the opportunity to work with the nursing faculty to redesign the college's administrative structure to include five associate deans. The associate deans had varied administrative experience, and each had a new set of responsibilities. We agreed to invest in our collective professional development and engaged Mary Connaughton to work with us in person two times a year in daylong retreats. In addition, Mary was available to talk with us by phone on a one-on-one basis to problem-solve issues that we were struggling with. The one-on-one conversations were treated confidentially. This coaching experience enhanced the team's resiliency and ability to work more effectively. It also provided us with the opportunity to regularly share with one another what we valued most about each other—helping us to better understand our strengths.

The sidebar provides reasons why you might want to consider engaging a coach. The remainder of this chapter provides an example of a coach's framework for working with clients. If you elect to work with a coach, it is important to consider the fit to optimize the experience.

TAKE ACTION: CONSIDER A CAREER COACH IF:

- *You aspire to a formal leadership role in practice or academia, yet question your readiness to be a manager.*

- *Despite many past successes, you are haunted by self-doubt.*

- *You feel stuck—torn between wanting to make a job change but terrified of leaving an organization after many years.*

> - *You are transitioning to a new job, and you need a confidential place where you can strengthen aspects of your leadership.*
> - *Your colleagues and family are always supportive, but now you feel the need to be challenged to stretch and grow.*

Build Your Model of Sufficiency

Over the course of Mary Connaughton's career, she has had the opportunity to engage in coaching relationships with many nurse leaders in practice and academia. Even some of the most accomplished leaders are more keenly aware of their shortcomings than their strengths. This turns out to be anything but a minor concern, dismissed as just a bit of insecurity.

You have the capacity for self-awareness, as well as the ability to access and leverage your strengths in any situation; this innate ability forms the bedrock of your confidence and fuels a belief that you can handle whatever comes your way. The best leaders are well versed in their unique talents and gifts, without arrogance. They are also aware of aspects of their leadership or practice that need further development, without self-criticism. Do we just give lip service to lifelong learning, secretly believing that this applies only to others while we expect ourselves to be perfect?

Dr. Angeles Arrien, cultural anthropologist, award-winning author, and educator, has studied indigenous people throughout her career in an effort to apply their ancient wisdom practices and principles to modern life. Her teaching and writing offer us powerful lessons in living our lives more fully and authentically. Arrien has special resonance for nurses who are often susceptible to minimizing their talents and contributions, thereby limiting the power of their presence and their practice. In her cross-cultural research, Arrien (1993) describes universal characteristics of people who are "at their best," or in their "full sufficiency," regardless of setting or circumstance. A four-point model of sufficiency, described in the next section, is based on Arrien's work. The model has proven to be an invaluable tool, especially when you find yourself susceptible to losing confidence in certain situations, including entering personal and professional transitions.

"OUR DEEPEST FEAR IS NOT THAT WE ARE INADEQUATE. OUR DEEPEST FEAR IS THAT WE ARE POWERFUL BEYOND MEASURE... THERE'S NOTHING ENLIGHTENED ABOUT SHRINKING SO THAT OTHER PEOPLE WON'T FEEL INSECURE AROUND YOU...AS WE ARE LIBERATED FROM OUR OWN FEAR, OUR PRESENCE AUTOMATICALLY LIBERATES OTHERS."

–MARIANNE WILLIAMSON (1996)

Self-Knowledge/Self-Awareness

Principle #1: Know your unshakeable strengths, those aspects of character, personality, experience, and skills that you uniquely bring forward and that never leave you, regardless of the circumstance. When in a challenging situation, being aware of your strengths will restore you to full sufficiency, or in other words, will ensure you are "at your best."

Reflection

- What are the unshakeable strengths that you uniquely bring to your work and personal life?

- When are you at risk for being unable to see or access your strengths? Do certain situations or personality types cause you to become insufficient?

Practice

- Make a list of your unshakeable strengths. (If you struggle with this, consult trusted colleagues, friends, or family members to share what they see in you.)

- Develop the habit of asking yourself, "Am I at my best?" as you prepare for a challenging situation or conversation. If the answer is no, take a moment to reflect on the strengths that will support you to handle whatever comes your way. "Come home" to your strengths and then march forward.

Principle #2: Rely first on your self-knowledge to see yourself, clearly identifying both the positives and areas of your leadership or practice that are not yet fully developed. This is where you are on the life and learning continuum. You are enough, worthy and deserving, just as you are. In your full sufficiency, you see the world through the lens of possibilities and abundance versus scarcity.

Reflection

- What are the messages you send to yourself? Is there a harsh critic whispering (shouting?) in your ear: "Not good enough, smart enough, thin enough..."?

- Do you find yourself frequently comparing yourself to others in a way that diminishes yourself?

- Are you prone to waiting for external validation or proof that you are OK, versus claiming what is within?

- What is your default position? "I can always find a way to make it work; I'll have what I need to be successful." Or, "I do not have enough time, energy, resources, or support."

Practice

- Pay attention to what you say to yourself. Make a daily habit of affirming your positive attributes and accomplishments.

- If you have a self-critical tape running through your head, turn it off!

- Appreciate and acknowledge others, while avoiding comparison. Aim to be the best you can be, versus aiming to be someone else.

- Consciously focus on what's possible and draw upon your creative spirit to manifest what you want, while dismissing fears of scarcity.

Principle #3: Aim for personal and professional excellence, not perfection. When you are at your best, you are clear-eyed both about your strengths and what you are working to improve. The clarity and self-acceptance that accompany this approach to life feeds the open, flexible, and forgiving places in our nature.

Reflection

- As you work to advance your education and potentially transition to a new role, to what degree are you in a learning mode, open to new ideas and points of view?

- When are you impatient with yourself or others? These are the situations where your intolerance or rigidity may stifle creativity and learning, for yourself and others.

Practice

- Assume a mind-set of curiosity when faced with differences or unexpected challenges, rather than assigning right and wrong: "Hmmm...I never thought about it that way before."

- Strengthen the practice of humility: "This is what I know; no one knows everything; I am open to discovering what others have to offer me."

- Be generous in acknowledging others, as we all need to be seen in order to thrive (Arrien, 2011). An abundance of genuine acknowledgement is an antidote to competition and the harshness toward self and others that accompanies perfectionism.

Principle #4: Accept responsibility for yourself and your self-care. When you are in full sufficiency, you will more readily accept responsibility for your thoughts and actions. We look first to ourselves in any situation, examining how we could have responded differently rather than judging and blaming others. We have a bias for action versus adding to the chorus of chronic complainers. Recognize that you must take care of yourself and not expect others to do this for you.

Reflection

- What is your typical reaction when a relationship with a colleague goes off track? Do you explore how you may have contributed to the misunderstanding? Or jump on the blame bandwagon?

- Have you become an expert at analyzing problems for others to fix? Or, do you come to the table with some possible solutions to problems you identify?

- Do you carve out time in your daily life to nurture your mind, body, and spirit? Or, do you tend to put everyone else's needs above your own, leaving your self-care to chance?

Practice

- Before you react, internalize the habit of pausing before judging or blaming, considering the possibility that you may have wittingly or unwittingly added to the problem by your action or inaction. Courageously owning your part paves the way for resolution with others.

- Commit to offering at least three possible solutions to every problem you identify. Your dedication to making things better will energize others to join you in shifting out of a complaining mode to an action mode. Chronic complaining is a bad habit that can be broken simply by choosing to take responsibility.

- Pledge to take an action every day that supports your health and well-being, whatever that means to you. A depleted, exhausted, dispirited nurse cannot be an effective healer or teacher. Assuming responsibility for self-care is an empowering step. It diminishes the tendency to try to hold institutions or other individuals accountable for your own happiness.

As you navigate through the process of advancing your education or making work transition decisions, do not underestimate the power of reflection. It is through reflection that you gain clarity about what you want, where your strengths lie, and how to effectively address the challenges you face. As with the kaleidoscope, you and the world are ever changing, but the constant is the beauty of your true nature. Everyone wants to be part of something bigger than oneself and to be able to leave a legacy that includes a belief that you gave it all you had—in other words, you lived your life striving to be in your full sufficiency.

References

Arrien, A. (1993). *The four-fold way: Walking the path of the warrior, teacher, healer and visionary.* New York, NY: HarperCollins.

Arrien, A. (2011). *Living in gratitude: A journey that will change your life.* Boulder, CO: Sounds True.

Williamson, M. (1996). *A return to love: Reflections on the principles of "A course in miracles."* New York, NY: HarperCollins.

"NEVER DOUBT THAT A SMALL GROUP OF THOUGHTFUL, COMMITTED CITIZENS CAN CHANGE THE WORLD. INDEED, THAT'S THE ONLY THING THAT EVER HAS."

–MARGARET MEAD

Chapter 2
Nursing Organizations 2.0

–Karen Grigsby

AFTER READING THIS CHAPTER, YOU WILL BE ABLE TO:

- Describe the benefits of joining a professional organization
- Identify which professional organizations fit personal career goals
- Describe the process of joining a professional organization
- Update your resume so that it includes the contributions you have made to nursing through your work in professional organizations

Nurses are educated to be lifelong learners. So as a graduate, how will you continue growing in order to advance your career? One of the most rewarding things you can do is join a professional organization. And the best news is that if you do this, you will grow personally as well as professionally.

Advantages of Joining a Professional Organization

There are multiple benefits to joining any professional organization. Attending meetings, reading journals that come with membership, working on committees–all of these activities expand your knowledge about issues impacting nursing and develop your leadership skills.

Participating in the work of a professional organization also helps you cultivate a network of colleagues while increasing your self-confidence. Finally, contributions you make to a professional organization should be included in your professional portfolio and/or resume. This demonstrates your involvement in the nursing profession beyond job responsibilities.

Whether you are a new graduate, an experienced nurse, or a nurse returning to school for advanced education, you need to seriously consider joining at least one or two professional organizations. Angela Barron McBride, distinguished professor and university dean emeriti at Indiana University School of Nursing, believes that each nurse should join two professional organizations: a nursing organization and an interprofessional organization (personal communication, September 19, 2012). Other nurse leaders believe that each nurse should join a specialty professional organization, such as the American Association of Critical-Care Nurses, and a more general professional nursing organization, such as the Honor Society of Nursing, Sigma Theta Tau International.

Whichever professional organization(s) you decide to join, it is important that you join to make a contribution. Joining to obtain a line on your resume is not adequate. When others review your resume, they will ask questions about your work for these organizations. Whether you are interviewing for a new position or for acceptance into a graduate program, your response will tell the interviewer about your interests and commitment to nursing as a profession as well as your dedication to achieving improvements in the health of others.

Joining and actively participating in professional organizations will give you the satisfaction of working to achieve its mission, while making a visible contribution to improving the health care available to others.

Matching Your Goals With the Right Professional Organization

Deciding which professional organizations to join can be difficult. The best way to approach this decision is to spend time reflecting on your strengths and the areas in which you want to make a contribution.

Begin by asking yourself some questions:

- What interests you the most about nursing and its mission?
- What are your strengths?
- What areas of weakness, or growing edges, do you have that need strengthening?
- What kind of a contribution do you want to make?
- What do you want to see as an outcome of your activities?

Record your responses as you reflect on the many areas of professional nursing where you can make a contribution. It might be helpful for you to write a personal mission statement. A personal mission statement will help you to focus on your strengths, your interests, and what contribution you want to make as a nurse.

Compare your personal mission statement to the mission and vision of each professional organization. Align yourself with an organization where you can apply your strengths and make a contribution. Examine your areas of desired growth and seek an organization that will provide support, experiences, and opportunities that will let you grow in the following areas.

Benefits of Organizations

- Collegiality
- Relationship building
- Mentoring and being mentored

- Networking
- Learning new knowledge and skills
- Leadership opportunities
- Making a contribution
- Increasing your self-confidence
- Career advancement
- Bringing fun and fulfillment into your life

Table 2.1   Deciding Which Professional Organization to Join

REFLECTIVE QUESTION	AREA OF FOCUS	SAMPLE ORGANIZATIONS
What interests you the most?	A nursing specialty	American Association of Critical-Care Nurses (AACN)
		National Association of Pediatric Nurse Practitioners (NAPNAP)
		Association of Women's Health, Obstetric, & Neonatal Nurses (AWHONN)
		Emergency Nurses Association (ENA)
	Professional nursing	American Nurses Association (ANA)
	Nursing education	National League for Nursing (NLN)
What contribution do you want to make?	Advancement of nursing knowledge	Midwest Nursing Research Society (MNRS)
		Eastern Nursing Research Society (ENRS)
		Southern Nursing Research Society (SNRS)
		Western Institute of Nursing (WIN)
		Council for the Advancement of Nursing Science (CANS)
		Honor Society of Nursing, Sigma Theta Tau International (STTI)

REFLECTIVE QUESTION	AREA OF FOCUS	SAMPLE ORGANIZATIONS
	Policy development	American Nurses Association Political Action Committee (ANA-PAC)
	Leadership development	American Organization of Nurse Executives (AONE)

Get to know organizations by:

- Asking colleagues about their organizational memberships

- Visiting the organization's website

- Inquiring about membership benefits

- Finding out if there is a local chapter

- Attending a meeting

- Volunteering for a committee

Remember that there are tangible and intangible benefits to membership in any organization. Whether you are receiving a journal, conference registration discounts, or the satisfaction of making a difference, being in an organization will help you grow personally and professionally. Finding an organization that fits your needs and goals and becoming an actively engaged member will help you advance your career.

What kind of experience helps you to build relationships best? Do you enjoy using technology, such as blogs and discussion boards, as a way to participate in an organization? Or do you find that face-to-face meetings are the best way for you to develop relationships and to feel connected to colleagues and to a professional organization? Your preferences are important as you think about the types of professional organizations you want to join, contributions you want to make, and learning experiences that you want to have. Reflecting on these questions will give you another decision point as you identify which professional organization is the best one for you.

IN REAL LIFE: KAREN GRIGSBY

It has always been important to me to give back to others. I was blessed to be mentored by some wonderful leaders throughout each stage of my career. Each of them taught me how important it was to give something to other nurses to help them grow professionally. They taught me how to dream and how to turn a dream into reality. Finally the day came when I realized that it was my turn to mentor others and to select where I wanted to make a contribution through serving in a professional organization. I made a deliberate decision to become more active in Sigma Theta Tau International. This was the organization where I thought I could make the best contribution. I liked the mission and vision of the organization: "to support the learning, knowledge, and professional development of nurses committed to making a difference in health worldwide" and "to create a global community of nurses" My passion has been to develop the next generation of nurse leaders who can develop and apply knowledge to promote the health of individuals through improving systems of care delivery. It was a good match for me. So I began to work at the chapter level and then at the regional level and then at the international level. I still continue to serve within this organization. It is a rewarding experience to foster the development of members while furthering the development of the organization as a global entity.

Join a Professional Organization

You have made your decision about which professional organization(s) to join. This is a critical step in advancing your career. So what do you do next?

- Check the requirements for membership. Some organizations, such as the American Nurses Association, only require you to be a nurse. And there are some organizations, such as the Honor Society of Nursing, Sigma Theta Tau International, that select members while nurses are enrolled in an undergraduate or graduate nursing program. If you were not selected for membership while you were a nursing student, there is still a place for you to join this organization. Sigma Theta Tau has a membership application entry for nurses in practice: Nurse Leader.

- Complete the membership application. Most professional organizations have an application for membership on their website.

- Some organizations require a member to nominate you for membership. Identify someone who is a member of the organization and ask them to nominate you for membership.

GOOD TO KNOW:

Here are some links that list numerous nursing organizations:

www.nurse.org/orgs.shtml
www.theagapecenter.com/Organizations/Nursing.htm
dir.yahoo.com/health/nursing/organizations/?b=20
en.wikipedia.org/wiki/List_of_nursing_organizations

Keeping Your Resume Current

Once you have joined one or more professional organizations, it is important to update your resume. Potential employers review your resume to decide if they want to interview you for a position, especially a leadership position. If you decide to apply to graduate school, this is also a time when you need to be sure your resume clearly describes your engagement in professional organizations. Leaders will review your resume to identify your contributions to nursing as a way to assess your potential as a leader and your commitment to the nursing profession.

EXAMPLE OF RESUME STATEMENTS

Date	Role	Professional Organization
2007–present	Member	American Nurses Association
2008–present	Member	Honor Society of Nursing, Sigma Theta Tau International
2009–2010	Chair	Membership Committee, Chapter Level
2010–2012	Vice President	Chapter Level
2010–2012	Member	Mentoring Counterpart Regional Committee

Once you have gained membership to one or more professional organizations of your choice, you have taken an important step in advancing your career and making a contribution to the nursing profession.

Use this checklist to systematically work toward making a decision about which professional organization is the right one for you.

❑ Know personal strengths.

❑ Identify desired contributions to make.

❑ Describe professional skills to develop.

❑ Write a personal mission statement.

❑ Identify several professional organizations of interest.

❑ Compare personal mission statement to the mission statements of each professional organization.

❑ Select professional organizations that match personal mission statement.

❑ Explore the membership requirements of each professional organization of interest.

❑ Complete a membership application for one or two professional organizations that are the best fit.

❑ After being accepted as a member of the professional organization(s), plan to attend meetings regularly.

❑ After attending several meetings, volunteer to serve on a committee as a way to become more actively involved.

Additional Reading

Dickenson-Hazard, N. (2008). *Ready, set, go lead!* Indianapolis, IN: Sigma Theta Tau International.

McBride, A. B. (2011). *The growth and development of nurse leaders.* New York, NY: Springer Publishing.

Saison, J., Smith, M., & Kemp, G. (2013). *Volunteering and its surprising benefits: Helping yourself while helping others.* Retrieved from www. helpguide.org/life/volunteer_opportunities_benefits_volunteering.htm

IF YOU LIVE LONG ENOUGH, YOU'LL MAKE MISTAKES. BUT IF YOU LEARN FROM THEM, YOU'LL BE A BETTER PERSON. IT'S HOW YOU HANDLE ADVERSITY, NOT HOW IT AFFECTS YOU. THE MAIN THING IS NEVER QUIT, NEVER QUIT, NEVER QUIT.

–BILL CLINTON

Chapter 3

Let Your Light Shine: Portfolio Principles

–Minna B. Masor

AFTER READING THIS CHAPTER, YOU WILL BE ABLE TO:

- Differentiate between a resume and curriculum vitae
- Understand the necessity of a portfolio
- Define a professional nursing portfolio
- Describe the components of a professional portfolio
- Identify different portfolio styles
- Create a professional portfolio

The Value of a Portfolio

Baby boomer nurses remember the days when it wasn't necessary to have a resume to get hired in just about any health care setting.

Times have changed. Nurses are on the same playing field as every other job seeker, whether engineer, accountant, or editor. To gain entry into a future employer's office, you must use the same career advancement tools, including LinkedIn and professional networks.

The time-honored resume is only the first tool to prepare and use in the journey toward career or educational advancement. Once you have a potential employer's attention and an interview is secured, a professional nursing portfolio can help demonstrate that you are the right person for the job and get you hired.

Here are some helpful definitions as you progress through the chapter and begin to formulate your own portfolio.

A portfolio is a collection of documents or selections of your work (Johnson, 2012). The origin of the portfolio dates back to 1722 Italy. The Italian translation is portafoglio: portare, which means to carry, and foglio, which means leaf or sheet (Portfolio, n.d.).

A resume is defined as a summary of one's accomplishments. It is a brief document that summarizes your education, employment history, and experiences that are relevant to your qualifications for a particular job to which you are applying (PurdueOwl.com, 2012).

The purpose of a resume (along with your cover letter) is to get an interview. The origin appears to be derived from the French word resumer: to resume, or summarize (Resume, n.d.). Components of a resume may include:

- Focused objective
- Summary of expertise
- Brief work history
- Education (formal and informal)
- Licensure and certifications

Based on these essential components, an early-RN-career resume could look like Figure 3.1.

FIGURE 3.1

RN Name, Credentials
Address
City, State Zip Code
Contact Number
Email@.com

OBJECTIVE: Seeking a challenging nursing position that will require me to expand my skills and practical experience while providing quality health care to patients.

EDUCATION: **Rush University, Chicago, Illinois**
Bachelor of Science, Nursing, Cum Laude, June 1997

Professional Licensure
Professional Nursing License #

Computer Experience/ Health Care Applications:
Windows XP, Microsoft Office (Outlook, Word, Excel, PowerPoint), Powerchart, Patient Care Information Systems

ACLS and BLS Instructor Certified
CCRN Certification

WORK EXPERIENCE:

June 1997- **Hospital Name – City, State**
Present *Title-Unit*
Responsible for assessing patient status from admission throughout hospitalization and surgical recovery. Plan delivery of nursing care for patients in coordination with the health care team. Charge role responsibilities include staffing, patient acuity level, and conflict resolution.

November 1995 - **Hospital Name – City, State**
June 1997 *Nursing Assistant II, Ambulatory Surgery*
Responsible for vital signs, assessments on postoperative patients, focused charting on progress towards discharge, discharge teaching, and stocking of supplies at bedside.

RECOGNITION/AWARDS

- Patient Safety Award – AIMMC – June 2007
- Rush Unit Advisory and Education Committee Member – October 1997 - July 1999
- Chicago Marathon Medical Volunteer – 1995 - Present

PROFESSIONAL ORGANIZATIONS

- Sigma Theta Tau International Member – Omicron Delta Chapter – June 2007
- Critical Care Nurses Association – 2006 - Present

A curriculum vitae (CV) is defined as an account of one's career and qualifications. A CV is a more detailed synopsis of your background and skills compared to the resume. The origin is from the Latin phrase "course of one's life." Topics found in both a resume and CV are similar to those found in a portfolio and may include:

- Educational and academic backgrounds
- Dates
- Program of study
- Internships/fellowships
- Teaching and research experience
- Publications
- Abstracts
- Podium presentations
- Research articles
- Presentations
- Formal
- Informal
- Awards
- Honors
- Affiliations
- Appointments

What Is a Nursing Portfolio?

IN REAL LIFE: MINNA B. MASOR

After completing my master in nursing degree, I was ready for a job as a nurse educator. As I began applying for positions, I realized I needed a way to bridge my years as a critical care nurse and my schooling to show I was a competent educator. I did not know where to begin. At the same time, I was moving to a new condo and needed to clean out my office. I started making piles of what to keep of personal, professional, household papers, etc. The professional pile kept growing so I began organizing the mass quantity of "artifacts" into different categories in a binder. I realized what I created was my first portfolio. My portfolio has changed over the years but is an amazing tool I use for interviews, self-reflection, and goal setting. It keeps me focused on future goals. The portfolio has been an invaluable tool along my nursing journey.

Most people are familiar with an artist's portfolio, which contains samples of works of art collected in some type of portable binder, or a writer's portfolio, which consists of samples of published works. The professional nursing portfolio adds depth to your interview and allows you to stand apart from the other candidates. It helps tell your story and enhances the standard resume.

The nursing portfolio encompasses components of your skill level, evaluations, academic and professional achievements, as well as recognitions. It is a map, of sorts, of your nursing career.

In 1995, the United Kingdom made the professional portfolio a requirement for nursing practice (Casey & Egan, 2010). The United Kingdom feels that portfolios offer many benefits for both personal and professional development. Other countries, including Canada and New Zealand, also require a professional portfolio.

With the many health care changes occurring in the United States, some states may adopt the mandatory portfolio for relicensure (Johnson, 2012). In fact, a web search of nursing programs reveals that both undergraduate and graduate levels use the student portfolio throughout their curriculums.

A portfolio's content is a collection of documents gathered from different sources and can be in a variety of formats. The specific contents depend on the intent or purpose of the portfolio. Most portfolios will have the same basics, such as resumes, licenses, and certifications. But depending upon the focus or intent, the additional topics will change. For example, if you are a medical-surgical nurse looking to move into critical care, your portfolio may include case studies of the more complex patients cared for, along with outcomes. If you are a critical care nurse looking into a leadership role, you may want to include not only case studies of complex care and multidisciplinary rounds, but any committee activities that show solid critical thinking along with strong decision-making skills. A portfolio needs to be more than just a document that contains everything you have done.

If you use a CV instead of a resume, the CV will parallel your portfolio with similar topics. However, the portfolio gives life to those topics. It is an ever-changing, living document that details achievements over time. A portfolio serves multiple purposes. In addition to helping you secure your next position, it helps you reflect on your professional growth and development in order to assess the goals you have accomplished to date or to map out future goals. A portfolio can also be an assessment tool for identifying your strengths and weaknesses at a specific career point (Oermann, 2002).

Table 3.1 shows a variety of tabs and content that can go into a portfolio. The content does have some overlap to the resume and/or CV and can be adjusted depending upon your audience or use of the portfolio. By no means is this list all inclusive. The components that go into a portfolio are sometimes called artifacts (Bastable, 2008). Artifacts are often associated with archeological digs and are used to piece together the past in order to tell a story about a particular population at a given point.

The advantage of creating a portfolio is having an additional tool to tell your individual nursing story. For those of you who are more analytical in nature, the portfolio is a document organized in specific categories to show outcomes. Selected categories can highlight your talents (e.g., presentations and publications show speaking and writing abilities). No matter what the intent of a portfolio, it should emphasize your professional skill level at a given time.

Table 3.1 Tab Titles and Content Examples

TAB TITLES/HEADERS	CONTENT EXAMPLES
Introduction	Who are you? A brief personal statement of who you are today and an objective statement Goals Plans Mission
Resume or Curriculum Vitae	Committees and Committee Activity

TAB TITLES/HEADERS	CONTENT EXAMPLES
Licensure/Professional Credentials	Certifications BLS/ACLS/PALS American Nurses Credentialing Center Specialty Organizations

Education	Formal:
	    Academic Transcripts
	Informal:
	    Conferences
	    Continuing Education
	    Learning Management Transcript

Accomplishments/Awards	Professional Nurse of the Month Panel Participant Annual Safety Recognition Personal 2 Quotes in *A Daybook for Nurse Educators*
Appointments	Committees Volunteer Organizations
Research/Publications	Abstracts Investigational Review Board Proposals Grant Applications
Presentations/Writing Samples	Summary of Courses, Programs, or Projects Developed Curriculums Syllabi Case Studies (identifies critical thinking capabilities) Exemplars Brochures

continues

continued

TAB TITLES/HEADERS	CONTENT EXAMPLES
Competencies	Areas of Clinical Expertise
	Skill Checklists
	Evaluations
	Supervisor
	Peer
	Program
Professional Associations/ Activities	Chair Positions
Letters	Patient Thank-You
	Colleagues
	Professional
Miscellaneous	Job Description(s)
	Health Records

(Casey & Egan, 2010; Johnson, 2012; Oermann, 2002)

GOOD TO KNOW:

In the Institute of Medicine's 2011 report The Future of Nursing: Leading Change, Advancing Health, *the portfolio is highlighted for the advanced practice nurse. It is the IOM's recommendation that the APN use the portfolio as a way to document competency in order to sit for examinations (pp. 336 and 339).*

The Advanced Portfolio

If you are an advanced practice registered nurse, your portfolio will include sections on projects that specifically focus on a particular patient population and the outcomes of implementing evidence-based research in the care you deliver. For example, a nurse anesthetist will have a section on the types of cases performed along with agents used, as well as physician evaluations on collaboration. The critical care APRN will have a focus on dealing with the complexities of the critically ill patient, along with projects or research that impacted outcomes for the unit(s). As mentioned earlier, a portfolio is an evolving document that not only will change with your shift in specialty and role, but will also evolve based on the purpose it is going to serve.

My own portfolio as a stroke program coordinator has evolved over time and includes the foundations of a CV, licensure, and certifications, as well as a section on patient education. I provide sample materials developed for patients and their families, along with presentations I have done in the community for stroke awareness.

The changing portfolio can be compared to the differences in use between a resume and CV. The content of each is based on intended use. Here are examples of content with a specific intention:

- Documenting the ability to develop an education program
  - Formal presentation
  - Evaluation summary from the attendees
- Performance
  - Annual reviews
  - Peer reviews
- Documented skill level
  - Competency checklist
  - Self-evaluation
  - Expert evaluation

In fact, as I sit here and write this chapter, I see changes that I want to incorporate in my portfolio in order to truly reflect what I am doing today and what I have accomplished over the past year. For instance, when I first started out as a clinical instructor, my layout functioned more as a roadmap of work history and educational growth that slowly evolved to show how the two merged and supported course development and some of the committee work I took on. Today, I continue to lead with my professional summary. Here is a list of the tabs and content of my current portfolio:

1) *Curriculum Vitae*
   a. *Professional profile*
   b. *Professional work experience with bullets highlighting key roles and/or accomplishments under each position*
   c. *Education*
      i. *Formal with GPAs*
      ii. *Professional courses*
      iii. *Computer training/ applications*
   d. *Certifications*
   e. *Recognition and awards*
   f. *Professional organization*
   g. *Appointments*
   h. *Course development*
2) *Licensure*
   a. *State(s) licenses*
   b. *BLS and ACLS instructor cards*
3) *Letters/Awards*
   a. *Letters from patients, families, students, and colleagues*
   b. *Certificates for participation in panel discussions*
   c. *Awards*
   d. *National certification certificates*
4) *Continuing Education Programs*
   a. *Track for state licensure and national certification*
   b. *Track for disease-specific care program management*
5) *Publications*
   a. *Formal peer-reviewed journals*
   b. *Abstract presentations*
6) *Evaluations – My passion is teaching, so I include evaluations of programs I have presented in order to show areas in need of development or adjustments in content.*
7) *Patient Education*
   a. *Materials on types of strokes, risk factors, and modifiable behaviors*
   b. *Presentations for the community to educate families and neighbors*
   c. *Patient Satisfaction results*
8) *Presentations – This is where I highlight various programs I have created and presented.*

The Electronic Portfolio

Technology is steadily and systematically being integrated in all aspects of health care, bringing with it the concept of an electronic or e-portfolio. Although more seasoned nursing professionals may prefer a hard copy portfolio, it is more time consuming to update. An e-portfolio can improve efficiency, store data with time stamps, and serve as an online tool for marketing yourself. The e-portfolio has gained popularity over the years and is also used by teachers, students, and artists. The content in an e-portfolio is not different from the paper form; it is just housed and categorized using many media formats (Barrett, 2001).

The e-portfolio still holds the numerous artifacts but "in many media types (audio, video, graphics, text)" (Barrett, 2001, p. 2). A benefit of the e-portfolio is that its web-based nature makes it accessible from any computer. It can also be viewed more thoroughly by the interviewer because it can be left behind after the interview. If you are not comfortable with technology, an option is to use a flash drive to store all the artifacts. You can take the flash drive into the interview, and the artifacts will be readily available should something be needed. Creating an e-portfolio can be a daunting task, especially when thinking of how to categorize your artifacts in an electronic format.

As I was researching material for this chapter, I came across the use of e-portfolios in a significant number of undergraduate and graduate nursing programs as well as professional nursing organizations. As a member of the Honor Society of Nursing, Sigma Theta Tau International, I have access to a specific template called Critical Portfolio (there is an annual fee for this service). Critical Portfolio, which is also the official platform for e-portfolio services of the American Nurses Credentialing Center, goes beyond the conventional curriculum vitae. More information can be found at http://www.nursingsociety.org/Career/CareerMap/Pages/critical_portolio.aspx (Sigma Theta Tau International, n.d.).

Portfolio Designs

One of the initial formats of a nursing portfolio is the hard copy. Hard copy portfolios are somewhat standard and may be developed using file folders, a three-ring notebook, or a scrapbook with copies of pertinent information inserted. As mentioned earlier, the pieces of pertinent information are often referred to as artifacts (Bastable, 2008). The word artifact is perfect for this medium, as it describes and documents your professional progression. Hard copy portfolios are the easiest to build, but time consuming to update.

Portfolios can be as straightforward as mine in a white, three-ring binder with a simple cover sheet. For me, this type works and fits my personality. I have also seen creatively decorated scrapbook portfolios. The design and format are personal decisions, but need to reflect who you are and what your purpose is. I use colored file folders to house all of my artifacts, which allows me to add or remove items from my binder. I do use a flash drive to back up some of the more critical components, such as my resume and CV, as well as published materials.

When to Use a Nursing Portfolio

The portfolio should be used in interviews. The newly licensed nurse (NLN) can use the portfolio to highlight group projects that exhibit teamwork or to show evaluations from clinical instructors on their performance. The more experienced nurse can use the portfolio to show documentation of competency with a skills checklist or share project management skills with unit initiatives and outcomes.

Portfolios offer an additional benefit during the interview process. They can alleviate interview anxiety and guide your answers if you are drawing a blank to a particular question. Often, you are nervous or unable to formulate an answer, increasing your own anxiety. You can refer to sections of your portfolio to support your interview process.

IN REAL LIFE: MINNA B. MASOR

I was in a group interview and was an absolute nervous wreck. But I wanted to make a good impression because I really wanted this position as a nurse educator. One question was particularly difficult, so I reached down and pulled my portfolio onto the table. Not only did this allow me to move to the achievements section and more

*clearly articulate the outcomes of a particular education program
I put together, but the brief break also allowed me to take a deep
breath. This eased my anxiety, and I saw I had captivated the group
with my portfolio. I did get the position, and I set a standard for all
incoming candidates to bring a portfolio to the interview.*

TAKE THE TIME TO CAREFULLY AND OBJECTIVELY EVALUATE THE CONTENT
OF YOUR PORTFOLIO TO ENSURE IT FITS YOUR CURRENT PURPOSE.

Advantages of the Nursing Portfolio

When used as a tool for reflection, the portfolio can keep you engaged in the
self-learning process. Benefits include:

- Self-enlightenment

- Career enhancement

- Record of growth and development

- Record of performance over time

- Tool for planning

- Fun to create

- Can act as a resource for others looking to create one

(Casey & Egan, 2010).

Ready, Set, Go Create Your Portfolio

As nurses, we are familiar with the nursing process. The professional
portfolio can be developed using a similar process that is focused on structure
(Overgaard, 2010). The creation of a document or program like a portfolio
can also be looked at as a project. Both the nursing process and project
management take a focused approach to get an end result or outcome
following a set of steps.

As the nursing process revolves around a patient's problems, a project is
built around the same framework of having a problem and needing a solution.
The process employed by both project managers and nurses can be used as a
tool in any profession, allowing one to incorporate logic and objectivity into
every decision (Overgaard, 2010).

There is no right or wrong way for developing your nursing portfolio; the main thing is to do so in an organized fashion. Here is one approach to get you started:

- Decide on format design.

- Purchase the following:

  - Binder or other format for portfolio

  - File folders to organize the artifacts

  - Flash drive for extra storage capabilities

  - Binder dividers

  - Labels or a label maker for the dividers

- Create a worksheet or outline: This can have headings with specific questions or objectives and will act as the guide to the contents of the portfolio. This would be the assessment phase of the nursing process (refer to Table 3.1 on pages 34–36 for ideas).

- Assess the intent of the portfolio (still part of the assessment phase as well as initial aspects of planning).

- Develop a table of contents: This is really planning the overall content to be included and helps with organizing the artifacts. Remember, the table of contents is a fluid list and can change, depending upon the intent of the portfolio.

- Create the tabs from the table of contents. This falls into the implementation phase.

- Take all of the artifacts and begin arranging them in their appropriate section based upon topic.

- Evaluation is a two-part process.

  - Review the portfolio and ask if it makes sense as well as flows.

  - Put a second pair of eyes on the end result—this provides an objective view.

Regardless of your goal, you want your portfolio to help you stand out in the crowd of applicants. As mentioned earlier, the resume is the tool to get in the door for an interview. What the portfolio does is solidify during the interview that you are the best candidate for the position. And finally, the portfolio will show the progression of your growth within the organization and help as advancement opportunities arise.

IN REAL LIFE: MINNA B. MASOR

Several years ago I had hit a crossroads of sorts. I loved my amazing colleagues and the organization where I was working. I was in a quandary, though, as the role I had was not a "lock and key" fit for me. I was fortunate to have Donna King, my VP/CNE of nursing walk into my office to ask if I might be interested in taking on the stroke program for our organization. The hospital was ready to take the next steps necessary to gain Primary Stroke Center Certification but had a few hurdles to tackle. I was taken aback at first by my own fears but quickly jumped at the chance for a new beginning (and of course, a challenge). I know this was one of the best decisions I have made along my professional journey. Sometimes we don't want to see in ourselves what we can (or should) do, and it takes a leader to identify the next move to make. I am so grateful for the opportunity I was given. I get to come to work each day and do what I love: work hands-on with patients and educate and guide patients, nurses, and physicians on how we can continually improve the lives of our patients and families.

Good luck on the journey through your nursing career, and enjoy the process of developing your own portfolio to show off who you are.

References

Barrett, H. C. (2001). Electronic portfolios. In *Educational Technology Encyclopedia*. Retrieved from www.electronicportfolios.com

Bastable, S. B. (2008). *The nurse as educator: Principles of teaching and learning for nursing practice*. Sudbury, MA: Jones and Bartlett.

Casey, D. C., & Egan, D. (2010). The use of professional portfolios and profiles for career enhancement. *British Journal of Community Nursing, 15*(11), 547-552.

Hahn, J. A. (2011). Managing multiple generations: Scenarios from the workplace. *Nursing Forum, 46*(3), 119-127.

Institute of Medicine. (2011). *The future of nursing: Leading change, advancing health.* Washington, DC: The National Academies Press.

Johnson, J. A. (2012). The professional portfolio: A tool to document nursing competency. *Journal for Nurses in Staff Development, March/April,* 91-92.

Oermann, M. H. (2002). Developing a professional portfolio in nursing. *Orthopaedic Nursing, 21*(2), 73-78.

Overgaard, P. M. (2010). Get the keys to successful project management. *Nursing Management, 41*(6), 53-54.

Portfolio. (n.d.). In Merriam-Webster's online dictionary (11th ed.). Retrieved from http://www.m-w.com/dictionary/portfolio

Purdue Owl. (2012). Retrieved on 1 August 2012 from http://owl.english. purdue.edu/owl/resource/641/01/

Resume. (n.d.). In Merriam-Webster's online dictionary (11th ed.). Retrieved from http://www.m-w.com/dictionary/resume

Sigma Theta Tau International. (n.d.). The critical portfolio: Web-based portfolio management. Retrieved October 20, 2012 from http://www. nursingsociety.org/Career/CareerMap/Pages/criticalportfolio.aspx

Somers, M. M. (2002). The complete guide to resume writing for nursing students and alumni. Baltimore, MD: John Hopkins University.

Additional Reading

Hahn, J. A. (2011). Managing multiple generations: Scenarios from the workplace. *Nursing Forum, 46*(3), 119-127.

Somers, M. M. (2002). The complete guide to resume writing for nursing students and alumni. Baltimore, MD: John Hopkins University.

Chapter 4
Cultivating Recognition

–*Antonia M. Villarruel*

AFTER READING THIS CHAPTER, YOU WILL BE ABLE TO:

- Recognize barriers that impact receiving professional recognition
- Assess professional and academic trajectories and begin to set short- and long-term career goals
- Accurately review the nature of your contributions to ascertain where you are and help you determine the most appropriate award and the proper timing for application
- Develop a plan for professional and/or academic recognition
- Identify the most qualified peers and mentors to be your sounding board

Why Professional Recognition for RNs Is Necessary and Appropriate

All nurses at some point in their professional lives want and need to be recognized for their contributions, creativity, and impact on their patients or students, coworkers, and institutions. In your daily professional life, recognition and appreciation come from informal and often spontaneous exchanges. A verbal thank-you, a note or a token of appreciation, and a letter from a supervisor are all forms of informal recognition.

Professional recognition is a more formal acknowledgement of sustained contributions or effort. This type of recognition most often takes the form of nominations and awards at the institutional or professional level.

Within the educational or institutional setting, awards reinforce values and behavior that are consistent with the mission of the institution. To those outside the institution or organization, awards and recognition indicate outstanding talent and motivation. For individuals receiving the recognition, awards serve as important validation and affirmation of contributions and the impact of the work and its significance. This affirmation is important when considering promotion, appointment to professional and other leadership positions, and career mobility. Professional recognition is also a reflection of the setting, environment, and even the profession in which you work. Institutions take pride in the success of their employees, because it is an indicator of institutional excellence and affirms the values of the organization.

Despite the importance of professional recognition, there is little written about how to think about and plan for receiving it. This may occur in part because of beliefs that seeking recognition is self-serving; that is, if you were truly deserving of recognition, you would not need to plan to seek recognition nor ask for assistance in being recognized. Other beliefs that serve as barriers for women seeking recognition are the fear of appearing overly confident or vain (Moss-Racusin & Rudman, 2010) and expectations that women should be collaborative versus assertive and decisive (Rudman & Glick, 2001)

These beliefs are reasons why nurses, in particular, are reluctant to deliberately seek recognition or awards. This chapter describes how to develop plans for seeking successful nominations for recognition.

IN REAL LIFE: ANTONIA M. VILLARRUEL

*There have been several critical junctures in my career when people
I respected have provided critical affirmation and support. Early
in my career, I was trying to determine the best time to pursue a
master's degree. Several nurse educators I spoke with were less than
enthusiastic about my wanting to enroll in graduate studies, in part
because they thought I did not have sufficient clinical experience.
At my first meeting of the National Association of Hispanic Nurses
(NAHN), I asked Dr. Ildaura Murillo Rohde, the founder of NAHN
and the most influential Latina nurse I had ever met, about the
"right" time for graduate studies. When I shared with her my
experiences and what I wanted to do, her answer was, "My dear,
what are you waiting for? You need to do this now—and don't stop
at a master's degree!" In another example, I submitted my first NIH
grant when I was a first year post doctoral fellow at the University of
Michigan. I was devastated when my "pink" sheets came back and
my grant hadn't been scored. I took the "not discussed" as a sign
that maybe I wouldn't be a successful researcher. A few days later, I
received flowers with a note: "You have what it takes." The note was
from Dr. Nola J. Pender, associate dean for research and director
of the T32 postdoctoral program. These thoughtful acts were the
encouragement I needed to deal with the bumps in my career path.*

Developing Plans for Professional Recognition

The idea of seeking recognition should be viewed as more than personal
validation. Although important, professional recognition in the form of awards
and membership in certain professional societies, such as the American
Academy of Nursing and Sigma Theta Tau International, are also part of
a career development strategy. Career development or planning empowers
nurses to chart a professional path and take responsibility for careers by
developing a vision and realistic plan for the future (Shermont, Krepcio, &
Murphy, 2009). In this context, external awards and nominations serve as
outside validation of excellence and consistent contributions to the profession.

Creating Your Vision

A critical component in career planning and in seeking recognition is to create a vision for your professional career. For example, you should be reflecting on such questions as:

- Where do you want to be in your career in 5 years? Ten years?
- What do you want to be doing?
- What do you want to accomplish?
- How will you know if you are successful?

This vision is essential for creating a plan that ensures career development as well as professional and personal satisfaction. As the great philosopher and Hall of Fame baseball player Yogi Berra said, "You've got to be very careful if you don't know where you're going, because you might not get there" (Baseball Almanac, 2012, para. 30). In most instances, professional recognition will not be an end in and of itself but can serve as a means to support your career development.

Conducting a Self-Assessment

Another strategy that facilitates career planning and professional recognition is a critical and comprehensive self-assessment. Begin with a list of your personal and professional values. Although seeking acknowledgment may not be a stated value, professional advancement, integrity, and excellence are consistent with pursuing recognition. Understanding your values will help in determining the best venue or match with the goals of professional associations and specific awards from which you seek recognition.

There are several components to a self-assessment, including listing professional accomplishments and professional activities. A good way to start your self-assessment is by updating your curriculum vitae (CV) to make sure you have a comprehensive list of all your professional activities, such as membership in professional organizations, participation in committees and task forces, presentations at professional meetings, publications, media interviews, and development of specific media, such as a web page or blog.

Although this may be a relatively simple task, a more difficult task is reflecting on your specific contribution and the impact of your work. For example, you may have a comprehensive list of professional organizations or committees included on your CV. The question that needs to be asked is:

What was your specific contribution to the organization or committee? What specifically did you do that demonstrates your leadership or other unique skills? Belonging to an organization and attending meetings are different from leading a change or a specific initiative that showcases your skills.

Similarly, it is important to reflect and demonstrate the impact of your contribution. In other words:

- How did your contribution affect a wider institutional or system change? Who did your contribution affect?

- What evidence do you have that others have used or implemented your innovation in other settings? For example, while you may be a prolific writer and have an extensive publication record, evidence of impact would include the number of times your work has been cited, requests for you to speak and consult related to your expertise, and adoption of an innovation or process you led.

Some examples of impact can be seen in guidelines for applications for the fellowship in the American Academy of Nurse Practitioners (AANP) and the American Academy of Nursing (AAN) and membership in the Honor Society of Nursing, Sigma Theta Tau International. Becoming a fellow in the AANP, for example, requires evidence of impact on the nurse practitioner profession by conducting research, developing clinical practice models, teaching innovations, and influencing health policy (AANP, 2012). Examples of impact include influencing evidence-based practice standards, developing educational strategies that impact outcomes, and interacting with policy or decision makers to affect health policy.

Fellowship in the American Academy of Nursing requires consistent and outstanding contributions over time (AAN, 2013). Evidence of outstanding contributions includes activities or accomplishments with significant and measurable impact, dissemination and adoption of research findings, or innovations that guide changes in education and research. Membership in Sigma Theta Tau International as a nurse leader requires demonstrated achievement in nursing, such as creativity and innovation in clinical practice and leadership to improve clinical practice (STTI, 2012). Examples of leadership achievements include developing policy and procedures to improve patient care, developing patient care programs, and serving in leadership positions.

As part of your self-assessment, it is important to incorporate the views of your supervisors, peers, and people you respect in the field to help put in perspective the impact and uniqueness of your contributions. A common source of input often neglected in self-assessment is your annual performance review. You should reflect and examine your past evaluations to hear what your supervisors have noted as your strengths and contributions. It is important to list those as part of your self-assessment, even if you don't necessarily feel these are personal strengths. The same should also be done in relation to weaknesses or areas for growth. Although you may not agree, it reflects how other people see you. What are they seeing that you are not? How can you communicate to them—and others—the professional you are or want to be?

The review of your accomplishments and impact, such as those listed in your CV, is essential because most nurses are likely to underestimate their respective contributions. The underestimation is also likely to occur when an accomplishment is part of a team effort. A colleague or coworker who is familiar with your work can provide insight that will help you to define your unique contributions and to understand the impact of your work on others in the context of the organization and beyond. Similarly, colleagues could also suggest areas that you might need to work on in order to develop a successful nomination.

Developing a Plan

A comprehensive self-assessment is an important step in evaluating your potential for specific awards or recognition. A strategy would be to review your achievements in relation to specific award criteria, as well as the accomplishments of past awardees. This review will help you identify the experiences you may need to demonstrate your leadership and expertise. For example, you might look for opportunities to volunteer or be appointed to a committee that uses your expertise, or assume a leadership position, such as heading up a specific task force on a committee of which you are currently a member.

You may also need to communicate your accomplishments and impact to a wider audience within and outside your institution. Attending professional meetings where you can discuss and share your work in formal and informal ways is another important strategy. A formal method is to submit an abstract for a poster or paper presentation. Consider presenting your work at a local, national, or international meeting; write about your work in your institutional communications; and think about the appropriate venue to publish your work.

An informal method is to attend a meeting and to be strategic about the sessions you attend and the people you want to meet. For example, you might want to meet the author of a publication whose work is similar to yours. You might want to meet the president of an organization, an author of an article that has inspired you, colleagues who are doing similar work, or the dean of a particular school. Think about what you say to people you want to meet:

- What do you want them to know about you?
- What do you want them to know about your work?
- What do you want to share about the work they have done and its impact on you?
- What opportunities for dialogue or continued interaction would be useful to you or to them and their organization?

The important component about these encounters is that you want them to remember you and your work. For many, it is not about doing good work—it is about communicating the impact of your work. This won't happen by itself.

A critical step as you develop your plan is to "sense-check" your ideas and plans within your network. You might share your plans with trusted colleagues or a senior person whose work and career trajectory you have admired. In addition, a good time to discuss your ideas and plans is during your performance evaluation. Your supervisor is in a good position not only to provide feedback on your approach but also to create opportunities to facilitate reaching your goals. Again, it is important to be prepared to ask for what you need from your supervisor and others within your network, such as support, protected time, critical feedback, and introductions to others who might also facilitate your goals.

You must also be prepared to hear what others have to say, both positive and negative; think about it and decide how to respond to the comments. Although comments may initially seem negative, it is important to obtain insight on what additional evidence or activities might help in the development of a competitive nomination. Similarly, if people are positive, it is important to probe and raise questions that might have been a concern to you, so you can ensure you are getting the feedback you need.

Developing a Successful Nomination

As seen in the following exemplars, there are different pathways to developing a successful application for an award.

IN REAL LIFE:

Emily had a diverse nursing career in government and public health service. She was a recognized leader in health care but less well known in nursing. Several of her colleagues wanted to nominate her for a leadership award in nursing. Emily reviewed the nomination process and was concerned that she did not have evidence of impact of her contributions, since examples provided were more in line with leadership in an academic setting. In addition, Emily's employer, although supportive of the process, was not necessarily encouraging. After working on the application process for a while, Emily declined to be nominated.

IN REAL LIFE:

John had always aspired to receive a specific award for excellence in practice. He was encouraged by his manager to submit a nomination for the award, and his manager had identified several people to nominate him. The nominators wrote letters of support but did not review his application. John had applied three times but was unsuccessful. Discouraged and embarrassed, he vowed he would never apply for the award again. After a year had passed, he was again encouraged to apply by his manager. John sought out a colleague who was a past member of the awards committee. His colleague agreed to nominate him and review his application packet. She provided a thorough critique of his packet, and John had to restructure his CV and also his nomination statement. With the help of his colleague, John was successful in obtaining the award.

Regardless of the outcome in these exemplars, some critical elements in submitting a successful application include:

- Identifying the right award
- Determining the right time to submit a nomination
- Identifying the right nominators
- Writing and submitting a successful application

Identifying the Right Award

The right award is the award that is a match with your values, skills, and where you are in your career. Most often people do not go "searching" for awards, but rather know about specific awards from the organizations to which they belong, from professional and lay media, and from someone who has actually received a specific award.

A multitude of awards recognize many aspects of the nursing profession. For example, there are awards for early, middle, and late career contributions; awards acknowledging contributions in research, teaching, practice, and policy; and awards given by different professional and public organizations.

It is important in thinking about awards, whether you are pursuing an award or being asked to consider nomination, if the values of the organization are congruent with your professional and personal values. In other words, will the award be meaningful to you and your organization? If not, the time and effort involved in the nominating process may not be worth the investment. This was the case with Emily in the first exemplar. Although Emily's colleagues wanted to recognize her contributions to the nursing profession, this was not a priority for Emily or her organization.

Reviewing contributions and attributes of past awardees is one way to determine if the award is a good fit with your skills and values. Talking with someone who has received an award that you are interested in can provide valuable insights in determining the match of your accomplishments with the award.

Determining the Right Time to Submit a Nomination

Determining the right award will help clarify when the time is right to consider a nomination. As discussed earlier, it is never too early to think about or plan for recognition. However, the actual submission of a nomination is dependent on several factors. For example, there may be nuances to the actual award that might influence selection of recipients. Some awards, for instance, while honoring excellence in leadership, may have a special emphasis on recognizing a type of leadership (e.g., clinical practice, research, or policy), early career professionals, or individuals from a specific geographic or work setting.

This special emphasis might provide you with a slight edge or a particular disadvantage. Second, it is important to plan for enough time to identify nominators, if needed; write and complete the application; and obtain timely feedback and review.

Identifying the Right Nominators

As seen in the second exemplar, deciding who should nominate you is an important consideration. In John's case, he had nominators who were well known in the field but who did not know or could not speak in detail about his contributions. In addition, his nominators were busy and did not take the time to work with him in developing a successful nomination.

In selecting sponsors, it is important to determine their availability, enthusiasm, and commitment to support your award nomination. As seen in the second exemplar, there was a difference in the involvement of nominators for John—in part, because there was a lack of clarity about what was needed. It is important to be clear about what you are asking a nominator to do, how you might help them, and also what assistance you might need in the application process. A common strategy used in developing nominations is to have the applicant develop an initial draft of a recommendation. In this way, salient points and accomplishments are certain to be included. This gives the nominator a basis from which to add their perspectives and also, despite how enthusiastic they are about writing the nomination, decreases the burden sometimes involved in the process.

Writing and Submitting a Successful Application

There are several critical points to consider in writing and submitting a successful application. The first point is to understand and follow the directions. Although this may seem obvious, many people do not thoroughly read the application instructions, and their nominations are not considered because of issues such as length of application, incorrect grammar, timeliness of submission, and submission of all materials.

Second, it is important that there is congruence in all elements of the application. For example, your CV should match the accomplishments you talk about in your own nomination or in letters from your nominators.

All elements of the application should blend together well and serve as reinforcements of important points. Finally, as mentioned previously, writing about yourself and the impact of your work is not easy. For this reason, it is important to have colleagues who know of your work help you describe your work in a way that illustrates your unique contributions. Another strategy is to quantify your accomplishments (Dembling, 2011). For example, you might list a number of publications, the number of times cited, and the number and type of awards you received. This is not bragging—it is simply pointing out the evidence and helping reviewers form a favorable impression of you.

In summary, seeking or receiving recognition in the form of awards is an important component of professional development. In many instances, receiving an award doesn't just happen; you have to prepare and plan for it. The preparation and planning do not make you less deserving of the award; they simply ensure that you are putting your best foot forward.

References

American Academy of Nurse Practitioners (AANP). (2012). Becoming a fellow. Retrieved from http://www.aanp.org/fellows-program/becoming-a-fellow

American Academy of Nursing (2013). Pre-application self-assessment worksheet. Retrieved from http://www.aannet.org/assets/docs/2013%20 pre-application%20self-assessment.pdf

American College of Nurse Midwives. (2012). Honors and awards, ACNM fellowship. Retrieved from http://www.midwife.org/ACNM-Fellowship

Baseball Almanac. (2012). Yogi Berra quotes. Retrieved from http://www. baseball-almanac.com/quotes/quoberra.shtml

Dembling, S. (2011). Are men better at selling themselves? *GradPSYCH, 9*(4), 44-46.

Frey, B. S. (2007). Awards as compensation. *European Management Review, 4*: 6-14. doi:10.1057/palgrave.emr.1500068. Retrieved on 04/07/13 from http://www.bsfrey.ch/articles/458_07.pdf

Moss-Racusin, C. A., & Rudman, L. A. (2010). Disruptions in women's self-promotion: The backlash avoidance model. *Psychology in Women Quarterly, 34*(2), 186-202.

Rudman, L. A., & Glick, P. (2001). Perspective gender stereotypes and backlash toward agentic women. *Journal of Social Issues, 57,* 732-762.

Shermont, H., Krepcio, D., & Murphy, J. (2009). Career mapping: Developing nurse leaders, reinvigorating careers. *Journal of Nursing Administration, 39*(10), 432-437. PMID 19820525

Sigma Theta Tau International (STTI). (2012). Nurse leader membership criteria. Retrieved from http://www.nursingsociety.org/membership/applynow/pages/nl_memcriteria.aspx

Chapter 5

Igniting Your Cheering Section

–Katherine M. Arroyo and Janice Phillips

AFTER READING THIS CHAPTER, YOU WILL BE ABLE TO:

- Describe the purpose of recommendations in an application process
- Identify potential recommenders for different professional opportunities
- Provide recommenders supporting information to craft an effective recommendation
- Properly handle declined requests from potential recommenders

At many points in your career, you will need a recommendation or professional reference. Recommendations are usually required when you are applying for academic programs, scholarships, awards, employment, clinical ladder advancement, honor society membership, leadership positions, and grant funding, just to name a few. While the written application and an interview provide opportunities for you to highlight your attributes, the recommender supports you through a third-party endorsement.

Recommendations play a vital role in the application process and can often make or break the outcome. Endorsements that contain either vague "glowing generalizations" or even a hint of reservation can be equally damaging to an otherwise strong application. Thus, you will need to carefully consider who can provide the strongest recommendation for each opportunity.

GOOD TO KNOW:

Reference or recommendation? Although these terms are used interchangeably in the nursing profession, the format of the endorsement needs to meet the criteria of the specific application. It is the applicant's responsibility to select an appropriate recommender and provide him or her with the information and tools needed to construct a strong recommendation. Applicants should always read the directions thoroughly in order to help the recommender develop an appropriate and viable recommendation.

Recommendation Formats

Traditional recommendations are formal letters. However, changes in society and professional practice have contributed to a variety of recommendation formats. Written letters, checklists, and short-answer questions can be submitted via mail or email. The Sample Recommendation Form (Figure 5.1) reflects a graduate program recommendation form that combines Likert scale questions with open responses on specific topics. Likert scales measure responses such as "strongly agree to strongly disagree" in surveys.

FIGURE 5.1: Sample Recommendation Form

ABC University
Confidential Recommendation

Name of Applicant: Last   First   Middle   Previous
name(s)

Planned Program of Study: _____
By signing this form, I waive my rights to review this document. I understand that recommendations from friends, relatives, or coworkers/colleagues will not be accepted. Recommendations from places of employment must be from a manager or supervisor.

Signature of Applicant

To the Recommender
The above person is applying for admission to ABC University. We are interested in obtaining all information you think would be helpful in assessing this applicant's qualifications for admission. Consistent with the Family Education Rights and Privacy Act of 1974, this form will not become part of the permanent student record and will not be available to the applicant.

How long have you known the applicant?

In what capacity have you known the applicant?

Describe the applicant's strengths in relation to his/her scholarly potential.

_____

_____

In what areas will this applicant need to strengthen skills or abilities?

_____

_____

Overall Recommendation
❏ 4 Strongly recommend
❏ 3 Recommend
❏ 2 Hesitate to recommend
❏ 1 Do not recommend

Signature of Recommender   Date

Name of Recommender   Position

Institution/Employer   Telephone

Address

Summary Evaluation
Please rate the candidate in comparison to other individuals whom you have known in a similar capacity on the following characteristics: *continues*

continued

Proficiency in Clinical Work ❑ Superior ❑ Above Average ❑ Satisfactory
❑ Needs Improvement ❑ No Basis for Judgment

Comments _____

Ability to Work with Others/Exchange Ideas ❑ Superior ❑ Above Average ❑ Satisfactory
❑ Needs Improvement ❑ No Basis for Judgment

Comments _____

Written Expression ❑ Superior ❑ Above Average ❑ Satisfactory
❑ Needs Improvement ❑ No Basis for Judgment

Comments _____

Involvement in Professional Development ❑ Superior ❑ Above Average ❑ Satisfactory
❑ Needs Improvement ❑ No Basis for Judgment

Comments _____

Perseverance in Pursuing Goals ❑ Superior ❑ Above Average ❑ Satisfactory
❑ Needs Improvement ❑ No Basis for Judgment

Comments _____

Leadership Potential ❑ Superior ❑ Above Average ❑ Satisfactory
❑ Needs Improvement ❑ No Basis for Judgment

Comments _____

Creativity ❑ Superior ❑ Above Average ❑ Satisfactory
❑ Needs Improvement ❑ No Basis for Judgment

Comments _____

Ability to Handle Stress ❑ Superior ❑ Above Average ❑ Satisfactory
❑ Needs Improvement ❑ No Basis for Judgment

Comments _____

Overall Comments:

Adapted with Permission, Rush University College of Nursing, 2013

Consistent with the trend of behavioral interviewing, many organizations are using electronic survey systems to elicit feedback on an applicant's behavior traits. Some employers are contracting with human resource companies to manage the recommendation process, particularly for telephone recommendations, so the recommender has the additional challenge of not communicating with the hiring manager directly. Regardless of the format, the strategies to securing a successful recommendation are the same.

"Bank" Your Recommenders

Thinking about potential recommenders is best done prior to needing a recommendation. By planning ahead, you can avoid having to make these decisions under the pressure of a deadline. The "Recommender Bank" (Table 5.1) provides space to identify your potential recommenders and a focused list of those attributes and accomplishments that each recommender can best evaluate.

The most valuable recommenders are those people who can comment on multiple areas, such as clinical, academic, leadership, research, etc. You will want to rely on several recommenders to present your full "professional best." Your Recommender Bank should be reviewed and updated on a regular basis: at a minimum, after every academic term for students and annually for practicing nurses.

When selecting recommenders, it is most important to select individuals who can speak to your skills, abilities, experiences, contributions, and future potential to advance in nursing. This may mean calling upon someone from further back in your past, such as former nursing professors or employers. However, you should also have recommenders who can talk about your more recent experiences and capabilities. By maintaining a Recommender Bank, you have a current list of potential recommenders to draw from when an opportunity presents itself.

Table 5.1

RECOMMENDER BANK

NAME CREDENTIALS TITLE	CONTACT INFORMATION	LENGTH OF TIME/ CAPACITY KNOWN	AREA(S) ABLE TO ADDRESS (CLINICAL, ACADEMIC, LEADERSHIP, RESEARCH ETC.)	SPECIFIC SITUATIONS TO HIGHLIGHT	OTHER INFORMATION

The best recommenders are individuals familiar enough with you and your work to provide a credible, detailed, and specific evaluation. Paul Bodine (2010) states that most often, recommenders are asked to comment on topics such as:

- Growth and career progress

- Leadership skills

- Interpersonal and teamwork skills

- Analytical, academic, and professional skills

- Writing and communication skills

- Character and integrity

- Volunteering and social impact

- Initiative and creativity

- Weaknesses

- Goals and potential

In addition, nursing-related applications may require that the recommender specifically address your actual and potential contributions to the nursing profession.

Personal friends, clergy, relatives, and acquaintances are not typically appropriate as recommenders unless they can personally attest to your professional qualifications. It is also inappropriate to ask a subordinate (someone you supervise) to provide a recommendation unless it is for a specific award or honor for which the subordinate has particular insight. In general, supervisors, academic instructors, close professional colleagues, and mentors provide the strongest recommendations. However, Martin Yate (2011), an international expert on job searching and career management, cautions against asking your current manager or coworkers for a recommendation if you are currently employed for fear it may cost you your job. Thus, it is important to consider this factor if you are pursuing other employment.

IN REAL LIFE: KATHERINE M. ARROYO

As a student and novice nurse, I felt comfortable approaching mentors for recommendations. However, I really struggled with becoming comfortable updating my list of potential recommenders. We all tend to have "default" recommenders, and it is challenging to move from our comfort zone and approach new people. Over time—perhaps with some maturity—I realized that not approaching a "default" recommender was in no way being disloyal or disrespectful. Rather, it was a testament to the important role he or she played at that point in my career and a statement of my own professional growth.

Now as a more seasoned professional who spends significant time providing recommendations, I have learned the importance of declining requests for recommendations when appropriate. Although I have a responsibility to provide recommendations in my role as practitioner and faculty, I am not obligated to provide a recommendation to everyone who asks...or presumes.

One of the most challenging experiences occurred when a new graduate provided my name as a reference for employment without my knowledge or consent. The human resources representative (part of a third-party company, not the employer) contacted me by phone mid-workday, and I was completely caught off guard. I was unfamiliar with this specific employer and the patient care environment, and frankly, I had some concerns about the candidate. I did my best to gracefully and positively address the representative's questions, but both of us were obviously uncomfortable with the conversation. (The candidate ultimately was not offered the position.) I did speak with the nurse later and advised her about the importance of communicating with potential recommenders ahead of time, which benefits everyone involved.

Understand the Application

Prior to selecting a recommender for a specific opportunity, you must first understand the directions in the application:

- How many recommendations are required?

- What selection criteria are the recommenders expected to address?

- Are all recommenders expected to provide similar information, or are there distinct areas that each should address?

- In what format is the recommendation?

- Do the recommenders need to submit their endorsement (to you, or directly to the organization), or will they be contacted by the organization?

- When is the deadline?

Once you are clear on the selection criteria and process of the recommendation, you can move on to selecting an appropriate recommender.

Choosing the Right Recommenders

When considering a recommender for a specific opportunity, you must identify which person from your Recommender Bank is most suitable. First and foremost, you should ask the questions: "How well does the recommender know me?" and "In what capacity?" The recommender must be able to speak specifically to your skills, abilities, experiences, and other professional and personal attributes. Additionally, the recommender must be able to address the selection criteria while highlighting personal characteristics that make you a candidate worthy of consideration. The suitability of the recommender will also depend on his or her availability and ability to address the items outlined in the application.

Table 5.2 provides factors to consider in order to select a suitable recommender for specific professional nursing opportunities.

Table 5.2

KEY CONSIDERATIONS FOR SELECTING RECOMMENDERS

WHEN APPLYING FOR...	SELECT A RECOMMENDER WHO CAN...
Graduate Nursing Programs	Discuss your current and/or previous academic performance Speak of your potential to complete graduate studies Describe your verbal and written communication skills Highlight your desirable characteristics such as integrity, diligence, professionalism, and potential to advance the profession Express familiarity with your short-and-long term professional goals Describe opportunities for your personal and professional improvement
Employment	Highlight your work experience(s) Describe your work attendance, quality of work, ability to work with others, dependability, honesty, and integrity Provide examples of your work performance and related impact Articulate your reasons for seeking the employment opportunity
Promotion and Clinical Ladder Advancement	Articulate all areas listed under "Employment" Provide specific examples of progressive leadership and accomplishments in the clinical setting Describe your demonstrated abilities as a preceptor, leader, and role model Present evidence of your professional development

WHEN APPLYING FOR...	SELECT A RECOMMENDER WHO CAN...
Entry Into a Professional Society	Outline your contributions to nursing
	Highlight your academic performance such as GPA and recognitions
	Describe your potential for and ability to advance the mission and vision of the professional society
	Articulate your leadership ability
	Describe your previous honors, awards, and recognition
Awards and Recognitions	Discuss your service to the profession
	Provide specific examples of your impact on advancing clinical practice, nursing education, nursing research, and scholarship
	Describe your contributions as a nurse leader
	Offer specific examples of your accomplishments and recognitions by other entities
	Link your contributions to the essence of the award or recognition
Grant Funding	Describe your research experience(s) and areas of expertise
	Discuss your previous research funding
	Highlight your research preparation
	Provide evidence of your scholarly contributions such as presentations and publications
	Highlight your other desirable characteristics such as project management skills and ability to complete projects
	Discuss your suitability for the proposed project

Remember, your recommender should be able to provide the strongest recommendation for a particular area.

For example, a clinical practice supervisor may not be able to speak to your academic potential. However, you may consider providing this supervisor with additional insights and materials to help the supervisor provide a well-rounded recommendation. Once you have identified an appropriate recommender, you should approach the individual to determine his or her willingness to provide a recommendation.

Applicant Responsibilities

Throughout the recommendation process, you are responsible for making the job of the recommender as easy as possible. Preparation and organization are essential. Maintaining professionalism will increase the likelihood of the recommender providing an effective recommendation. Remember, you need a good recommendation, not just any recommendation.

You should always ask permission before listing someone as a recommender. This is a simple professional courtesy. It also provides several advantages, such as enabling requestors to prepare their thoughts, gather any related materials, and learn more about what you are applying for. It also provides you the opportunity to:

- Confirm the correct credentials and contact information for the recommender

- Judge if the recommender is available and willing to provide a strong, favorable reference

- Provide the recommender time to prepare his or her thoughts and not be caught off guard (particularly important when a reviewer will contact the recommender by telephone)

- Speak with the recommender directly about your interest in the opportunity

- Receive feedback from the recommender that may strengthen your application

Note that you should never assume that a recommender will always be willing to provide another recommendation in the future. Permission should be sought for each separate recommendation request. For example, even if a college professor previously provided a recommendation for a scholarship, you should seek permission again before listing this professor as an employment reference. In addition, if you apply for several opportunities within a short time frame, you should inform the recommender about all of them so that he or she can tailor the recommendation to the criteria for each.

As soon as you become aware of an opportunity, you should contact potential recommenders. The timing of a request is very important, because a recommendation given under pressure will never be as favorable. There is no standard minimum amount of notice, but the sooner, the better. Yate (2012) recommends that you identify potential recommenders at the beginning of any job search. In some instances, a recommendation is not required until a job offer is made. However, you should anticipate this request up front and prepare a reference list ahead of time. For other professional opportunities, such as graduate school, awards, and grants, you should request recommendations 1 month or more in advance.

Preferably, you should request permission during a scheduled personal visit or phone call. If it is necessary to send the request by email, it should be formatted as a business letter. Pay special attention to using correct letter etiquette, spelling, and grammar. Whether permission is sought in person or through email, you should provide all relevant information about the requested recommendation, including:

- Specific background information about the opportunity and why you are interested in applying:
    - Graduate school—name of school, type of program
    - Employment, promotions—position title and description, facility, department, client population
    - Professional societies—group name, mission, specific leadership role sought
    - Awards and recognitions—name of award, sponsoring organization, selection criteria
    - Grants—type, amount, selection criteria
- A brief description of the relationship between you and the recommender, including dates
- Why you chose this recommender. What criteria do you feel the recommender can highlight?
- Current resume or CV
- Personal goals statement, if appropriate
- Any required documents for the recommendation
- Complete any sections to be done by yourself prior to sending the materials to the recommender

Sample Recommendation Request

July 1, 2012

Dear Professor Smith,

I am writing to see if you are willing to submit a letter of recommendation on my behalf for a faculty appointment. I applied for a clinical instructor position at ABC University College of Nursing and have scheduled an interview at the end of July. This position has a strong appeal for me because I believe it will assist me in achieving my long-term goal of securing a full-time nursing faculty position. I am also drawn to this clinical instructor position because the candidate selected will have an active role in developing the simulation lab at ABC University.

Because you served as faculty advisor for my MSN Education Practicum in fall 2011, I believe you would be able to give a supportive evaluation of my clinical teaching abilities. As you recall, my project focused on developing scenarios for standardized patients and high-fidelity simulators to meet clinical learning objectives for NRS 504: Health Assessment and NRS 516: Pediatric Nursing. I also improved my ability to evaluate student performance and provide feedback through both written and verbal student clinical evaluations. My experiences with two challenging students—the student with limited English proficiency and the student who required a formal development plan to meet clinical objectives—were particularly significant in my growth as an educator.

Enclosed are the position description for clinical instructor at ABC University, my curriculum vitae, a copy of my teaching philosophy, and my final performance appraisal from my MSN Education Practicum.

Please direct the letter to Dr. Mary Jones, Dean of ABC University College of Nursing. The search committee requested that I bring the letter of recommendation in a sealed envelope to my interview on July 30, 2012. I would be happy to pick up the letter from your office at your convenience.

Thank you for your time and consideration. Please contact me at 123-456-7890 if there is any additional information you would find helpful.

Sincerely,

Jane Doe

- Include an addressed, stamped envelope, if applicable
- Contact information for both yourself and the recipient
- Deadlines
- Any other information that will assist the recommender in composing a strong endorsement such as:
  - Final course/clinical evaluation of student
  - Application essay
  - Professional portfolio
  - Grant proposal

This sample recommendation letter reflects the level of detail you can provide your recommender to make his or her process easier. As you can see, the request is very specific in describing what is needed and when it should be submitted. The writer also provides the recommender with a pleasant reminder of their previous experience together in support of the recommendation itself.

NOTES FOR YOUR RECOMMENDATION LETTER:

Contact the potential recommender as soon as possible.

Use the recommender's proper name.

Describe the opportunity and reason for applying.

Provide a description of your relationship with the recommender.

Highlight significant topics or situations that the recommender should mention.

Include supplemental materials that will assist the recommender.

Articulate the format of the recommendation, to whom it should be addressed, and deadline.

Include contact information.

Thank the recommender.

GOOD TO KNOW:

Providing a copy of the application, position description, selection criteria, etc., assists the recommender with using the correct "keywords" in the recommendation.

A recommender will also need to know if you have secured additional recommenders and if there is a specific aspect they have been asked to address. Some applications may require some synergy between the recommendations, while others may ask for distinct responses. Thus, a careful review of the application guidelines is imperative!

Communication between you and your recommender throughout the application process is essential but must remain professional. You certainly want to avoid pressuring or hounding the recommender, as the recommendation will not be as favorable. If you do not receive confirmation that the recommendation has been submitted, it is appropriate to telephone or email the recommender to inquire on the status of the recommendation and to confirm the deadline if necessary.

You should update the recommender on the progress of the application process, and also on the outcome—whether it is positive or negative. Finally, you should write each recommender a thank-you note. Although some experts feel that it is part of the job to serve as a recommender, a wise applicant understands that the time and effort spent crafting a positive recommendation deserve acknowledgement.

IN REAL LIFE:

For a Robert Wood Johnson Foundation Health Policy Fellowship application, a nurse secured three letters of recommendation. The recommenders were selected because each was able to address a different aspect of the applicant's professional career that matched the selection criteria. One recommender highlighted the applicant's scholarly and research contributions; one described the applicant's professional growth and contributions to nursing; and the third described the applicant's legislative work as an advocate to reduce health disparities in breast cancer prevention. All three recommenders received a copy of the application packet, a current CV, selections from a personal statement, and an overview of the applicant's short- and long-term professional goals. In addition, all parties communicated via telephone and email throughout the entire application process. This ongoing communication was critical in crafting a competitive application.

Handling Awkward Situations

Although it is uncomfortable, occasionally a recommender will decline your request for a recommendation. There are several reasons why this might occur:

- The recommender is uncomfortable recommending you, either for the specific opportunity or overall.

- The recommender does not have the time available to commit to a recommendation, even with sufficient notice.

- The recommender may feel he or she does not know you well enough to provide a fair evaluation.

Remember, if there is any hesitancy or a direct "no" to the request for a recommendation, it is best for you to approach an alternate recommender. If a potential recommender states that he or she is not the best person to complete your request (e.g., not as familiar with your work, accomplishments, or academic performance as another individual), you should take his or her word and gracefully move on. A recommender who is being honest that the recommendation will not be glowingly supportive is actually doing you a favor.

Although it is a challenge for you not to take a "no" personally, it is helpful to remember that most individuals who are providing recommendations have spent years building up their own professional reputation. The applicants they recommend will also influence their reputation, whether positive or negative. Wise recommenders will decline to write a lukewarm recommendation because this may compromise their credibility in the recommendation of subsequent applicants. Remember, anything less than a glowing recommendation is harmful to both you and the recommender.

IN REAL LIFE:

Six months after graduation, a novice nurse contacted her former academic advisor requesting a recommendation for employment. The graduate had no other academic relationship with the faculty member other than as an advisee. The advisor declined writing the recommendation because she had no way of evaluating either the graduate's clinical or interpersonal skills, which were the primary focus of the recommendation. The advisor suggested alternate faculty who had directly supervised the graduate in clinical experiences and offered to critique the applicant's resume instead.

Another challenging situation occurs when the recommender asks you to draft a letter for the recommender to review and approve. Bodine (2010) cautions that such letters may not be as objective, genuine, or even enthusiastic compared to a letter written by the actual recommender.

Application reviewers are often astute enough to sense that the recommendation was written by the applicant, which may eliminate you completely from consideration. Experienced reviewers can also discern when you and your recommender have not communicated sufficiently to compose a competitive application.

If asked to compose your own recommendation, you would be wise to inquire if additional information, such as personal goal statements, would be helpful for the recommender in his or her preparation of the recommendation. However, if the recommender still insists you compose the letter, it may be that he or she is hesitant or uncomfortable providing the recommendation. It is best to gracefully move on and find another recommender.

Confidentiality is another sensitive recommendation issue. It is not appropriate for you to ask to see the recommendation prior to it being submitted. A recommender should feel safe giving an honest evaluation of you and feel confident that the information contained in the recommendation will not be communicated elsewhere.

Most recommendation forms, particularly in academic environments, include a signed statement for you to waive the right to see the recommendation letter. Experts recommend that you always waive this right. If you feel uncomfortable doing so, it may be that you are concerned that the recommender will be providing a less-than-enthusiastic recommendation. Again, if there is any doubt on the part of either the recommender or yourself that the recommendation will be anything less than positive, you should consider a different recommender.

IN REAL LIFE:

A clinical manager adopted a personal policy not to provide a recommendation unless the applicant waives the right to see the application. Previously, an applicant he supported obtained a copy of the recommendation letter, and then submitted it for other opportunities without the knowledge of the clinical manager. When contacted by a later application reviewer, the clinical manager had to admit that he knew nothing about the applicant's interest in that particular opportunity. In addition to making both the clinical manager and reviewer feel awkward, this situation also reflected poorly on the applicant.

Social Media Recommendations

Securing recommendations is also being influenced by social networks such as LinkedIn, Facebook, and Twitter. LinkedIn, in particular, has emerged as one of the leading professional social networks for job searching. In addition to its networking capabilities, LinkedIn allows you to create a personal profile, post resumes, and request and post letters of recommendation.

After creating a personal account, you can send requests for letters of recommendation from people who know you best. The letters are posted on LinkedIn, where potential employers and others can review the recommendations as they consider you for employment, awards, and other recognitions. Robert Fraser (2011), author of *The Nurse's Social Media Advantage: How Making Connections and Sharing Ideas Can Enhance Your Nursing Practice*, provides a comprehensive and user-friendly discussion on social media, related benefits, and key issues.

You're Ready to Go

In closing, recommendations are a significant part of your application when seeking professional advancement and recognition. You should carefully consider which recommender can provide the strongest, most credible endorsement for each opportunity. By providing the recommender with the appropriate supportive information and maintaining professionalism, you will increase the chance of receiving a strong recommendation that does present your professional best.

You can find additional assistance with recommendations from your employer's human resources department, career websites, and local nursing schools. Most professional nursing organizations also offer career guidance and resources that can be helpful during any application process. You can also utilize these resources when you are planning to return to school for an advanced degree.

IN REAL LIFE: JANICE PHILLIPS

Throughout my entire career, I have been blessed with many dynamic mentors and role models, far too many to name. These role models and mentors provided the encouragement and support needed to advance my career and were more than willing to share their expertise and resources so that I might develop professionally. One of the most remarkable highlights of my career took place when Dr. Anne Belcher nominated me for the American Cancer Society Professorship in Oncology Nursing at the University of Maryland. I still recall the moment when she approached me about the prestigious honor. She had mentored me as a junior faculty and felt confident that I could benefit from the professorship and advance my research on health disparities. It was this opportunity that helped me to solidify my expertise in and contributions to the breast cancer arena at an early stage in my career. I am a firm believer that nobody gets to where they are unless somebody helps them. And while I have many role models and mentors to thank, I am also mindful of the scripture that says to whom much is given, much is required.

References

Bodine, P. (2010). *Perfect phrases for letters of recommendation.* New York, NY: McGraw-Hill.

Fraser, R. (2011). *The nurse's social media advantage: How making connections and sharing ideas can enhance your nursing practice.* Indianapolis, IN: Sigma Theta Tau International.

Yate, M. (2011). *Knock 'em dead: Secrets and strategies for success in an uncertain world.* Avon, MA: Adams Media.

Yate, M. (2012). *Knock 'em dead: Turn job interviews into job offers.* Avon, MA: Adams Media.

Additional Reading

Christenbery, T. L. (2012). Preparing BSN students for the doctor of nursing practice (DNP) application process: The faculty role. *Nurse Educator, 37*(1) 30-35.

Scheep, B., & Scheep, D. (2010). *How to find a job on LinkedIn, Facebook, Twitter, MySpace and other social networks.* New York, NY: McGraw Hill.

Schiavone, Kristyn, (2012, July 2). Risks & rewards of job referrals. *Chicago Tribune*, p 14.

"LIVE AS IF YOU WERE TO DIE
TOMORROW. LEARN AS IF YOU WERE
TO LIVE FOREVER."

–MAHATMA GANDHI

Chapter 6

Graduate School: Crafting Successful Applications

–Marcia Murphy, Barbara Kitzes Hinch, and Barbara Swanson

AFTER READING THIS CHAPTER, YOU WILL BE ABLE TO:

- Identify the timeline for the steps of the application process to graduate school

- Describe key points regarding the components of the application process to promote success

- Develop an admissions checklist to ensure that all components of the process are completed

- Understand the importance of interview preparation in the application process

Mapping a Strategy for the Application Process

IN REAL LIFE: MARCIA MURPHY

I began my career as a novice nurse at Rush Presbyterian St. Luke's Medical Center. I selected this system as my first place of employment because it had a model of nursing in place called "primary nursing." This model required the nurse to assume full responsibility and accountability for his/her patients. I believed that this type of practice would foster my socialization as a professional nurse. This turned out to be the case. A particular turning point for me during my first year of practice was interacting with practitioner-teachers. These were master's-prepared nurses who were responsible for teaching both the nursing staff and nursing students on the unit. I vividly recall one day on the unit when I felt overwhelmed managing a patient on a ventilator. The practitioner-teacher on the unit recognized this and helped me with the care of this patient. I learned quite a bit that day about the care of ventilator patients. I was so impressed and inspired with this practitioner-teacher that I decided this was a position that I would like to hold one day. After 1 year of full-time work as a nurse, I applied to graduate school. A couple of years later, I was working as a practitioner-teacher on the very same medical unit that I starting practicing on as a professional nurse!

Crafting a successful application to graduate school requires your time, focus, and organizational skills. Admission to graduate programs, including MSN, DNP, and PhD, are competitive. Therefore, you want to be thorough and thoughtful in your approach. You should consider applying to more than one graduate program so that you have options to consider. The program director or registrar's office of your targeted university may be able to provide acceptance rates. This is useful information for you so that your target programs are a match with your background and credentials.

Although application processes vary somewhat depending on the specific program, common components include:

- Application form
- Resume
- Graduate record exam
- Academic transcripts
- Letters of recommendation
- Essay
- Interview

As you target schools, it may be useful to set up a system such as a table or spreadsheet to list the admission deadline dates, along with the specific university's admissions requirements (Christenbery, 2012). This will help keep you organized. Plan on beginning the application process at least 6 months prior to the admission deadline. This will provide adequate time to coordinate and complete the various components of the application process. A sample timeline with common components of the application is illustrated in Figure 6.1. Note that the deadline for targeted school is January 2014, and you should begin process at least 6 months in advance of the deadline.

FIGURE 6.1

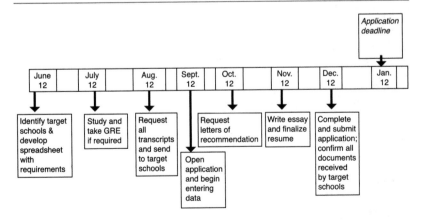

Four to Six Months Prior to Application Deadline

The Application Form

The application form is typically three to four pages in length. It includes personal demographic and background information. Plan a time to sit down and prepare this section without interruptions. All the information must be accurate and complete. Missing information may raise questions by the admissions counselors and committee. Also, the information on this form should be consistent with other documents being submitted, such as your resume. Discrepancies will also raise some questions and may not be viewed favorably.

IN REAL LIFE: BARBARA SWANSON

My scholarly development greatly accelerated when I began working as a research assistant for my dissertation advisor. As we worked together through every phase of her study, from project conception to final publication, I learned not only the "how to" aspects of research, but more importantly, the underlying processes that drove the science. I learned how interprofessional collaboration could redraw the original question, via an iterative process, to a highly specific question with clearly defined, specific aims. I learned how different data analytic approaches could yield entirely different answers to the research questions. I learned that there is rarely consensus among investigators about design, methods, analyses, and the meaning of findings. I learned that ambiguity is not an obstacle to discovery, rather it's a portal to new and unimagined discoveries. Most importantly, I learned that the journey of a scholar is never a straight shot, but a circuitous path characterized by unexpected detours that make all the difference.

The Resume

Your resume is a requirement of many graduate programs. It serves to provide the program faculty with a summary of your life experiences. Of particular interest to graduate faculty are leadership, scholarship, and community service activities. Chapter 3 describes the components of a good resume. The resume presents an opportunity to highlight your clinical and professional experiences in the best possible light.

Graduate Record Exam

Depending on the university and program, the Graduate Record Exam (GRE) may be a requirement. This standardized test aims to assess both verbal and quantitative reasoning, analytical writing, and critical thinking skills. Several schools have a certain cumulative grade point average (GPA) that may qualify you to have the GRE requirement waived.

Should your target schools require the GRE, you need to develop a plan to prepare for it. There are a variety of study strategies, such as review books, review courses, tutoring services, etc., that you should consider. Typically, an admissions committee will review and consider all components of the application, not just one piece of data, such as the GRE score. However, should this be a requirement, you will want to achieve a score that reflects your potential. This may require rigorous preparation.

Academic Transcripts

Graduate programs across the country will require you to send an official transcript from all the schools you have attended. This would include all previous academic work from every college or university that you attended, even if it is was one course taken at a community college. Therefore, it is very important that you begin this process early. Your application will not be reviewed by the admissions committee without submission of all your transcripts.

Less than Four Months Prior to Application Deadline

Letters of Recommendation

Letters of recommendation are an essential component of the graduate admissions process. As with the other aspects of the application process, carefully review the requirements of your targeted programs regarding criteria for the letters of recommendation. Typically, two to four letters of recommendation are required. A university may stipulate who should be targeted for the recommendation. For example, a recommendation from a nursing professor and a clinical nursing supervisor may be required.

These letters provide the admissions committee important information regarding your potential for success in graduate school. Many universities use a form for this letter that includes criteria, such as communication skills, leadership skills, and personal qualities. A letter of recommendation can illustrate how your personal qualities and experiences are a perfect match for the program to which you are applying. Therefore, it can provide the admissions committee with information that is not found elsewhere in the application.

The following list provides several important points to consider when acquiring your letters of recommendation. Ask someone who knows you well: The letters of recommendation can positively influence your status as an applicant. They provide a dimension of insight into your qualifications not attainable from transcripts and test scores. Therefore, it is very important that you ask people who know you well and have a high opinion of you. Consider college faculty members and clinical supervisors who directly know your work and achievements. They should also know you long enough to write with authority and credibility. You should aim for recommendation letters that cover the range of your skills, including academic work, clinical and research experiences, and leadership. Letters with specific examples and evidence of your work will be viewed as more credible by the admissions committee. Do not consider asking coworkers, friends, or acquaintances with doctoral degrees to write letters of recommendation. The admissions committee will not view these types of letters as credible. Table 6.1 summarizes suitable versus inappropriate recommender candidates.

Table 6.1   Who Should Write Your Recommendation?

APPROPRIATE PERSONS TO ASK FOR RECOMMENDATION	INAPPROPRIATE PERSONS TO ASK FOR RECOMMENDATION
Previous academic faculty	Coworker
Current clinical supervisor	Friend/colleague
Graduate-prepared nurse in the specialty you are seeking who knows you well	Acquaintance with doctoral degree
Chair of committee you are a member of	

Ask early: A letter of recommendation requires time and effort to write. Ask targeted recommenders for their recommendation at least 2 months prior to the due date. As faculty and others are barraged with requests to write letters, plan your approach thoughtfully. If possible, schedule an appointment to ask the person face-to-face. Bring to this meeting a summary of the degree that you are seeking, a list of your professional goals, and reasons why you believe this person is a good candidate to write a letter on your behalf. Consider forwarding your current resume and highlighting some of your recent experiences to your recommenders. This will enable them to write letters that provide actual evidence of your work and achievements.

Provide Essential Details

Many universities have an electronic system available for submission of letters of recommendation. Others still have the traditional letter that requires direct mailing. Provide the recommender with the specific information and material necessary to submit the letter of recommendation on time, including forms, electronic links, and/or envelopes with stamps. A more detailed discussion on selecting recommenders is located in Chapter 5. It is also important to communicate the due date for the letter of recommendation.

The Essay

Most graduate school applicants look similar to program reviewers. Typically, they have high GPAs and GRE scores and glowing recommendations. Your challenge is to distinguish yourself from the rest of the applicant pool by convincing the reviewers that you are a "must have" student. Surprisingly, this is not a difficult task and can be achieved through the personal essay. Every graduate program asks applicants to write a personal essay. And because program reviewers place a high value on this essay, you have a golden opportunity to sell yourself.

The personal essay opens a window that allows reviewers to glimpse parts of you that cannot be seen in test scores or transcripts. A well-written essay shows reviewers that you possess the attributes necessary to complete a rigorous program, that you will make a lasting contribution to nursing science, and that they will be proud to count you among their alumni. Additionally, it can even offset certain limitations in your application, such as a less than stellar GPA. So what are the elements of a personal essay that will move you to the top of the applicant pool? The acronym STOP will help you remember the elements of a successful essay: Before you submit your essay, STOP, and consider the following points.

- Singularity
- Tailored
- Organized
- Professional

Singularity

Your essay should convey the singularity, or remarkableness, of both you and your area of interest. Now, it is a fine line between being boastful and conveying your singularity, but you can walk this line without crossing it. Look at the example of an effective essay written by an applicant to a PhD program (Figure 6.2). The writer used what we call "startle statistics" to convey the importance and urgency of the research topic. The reviewers will quickly understand that this is a high-priority research topic and that the findings will likely inform the development of subsequent studies. Additionally, in just a few sentences, the writer made it crystal clear that he or she has the expertise and access to participants to complete this project. In contrast, the ineffective essay cites no data to support the research topic; its importance seems to stem only from the applicant's personal experience (Figure 6.3).

Tailored

Your essay should be tailored to emphasize the match among your skills, experience, and scholarly interests, as well as your program faculty expertise. If you are applying to a doctoral program whose faculty conducts clinical research to improve patient outcomes, that's the type of research project that you should write about. Do not write about theory-testing studies or studies to improve clinical skills in nursing students. If those are your interests, find a program whose faculty members have that expertise. An otherwise outstanding applicant can be denied admission if there are no faculty members with matching expertise.

Organized

Your essay tells reviewers how you think. It is important that your ideas are clearly stated and flow logically. Look at the ineffective essay (Figure 6.3). The applicant's initial sentences suggest a lack of sophistication and provide neither an introduction nor context to the research topic. In contrast, the writer of the essay in Figure 6.2 provided both rationale and context in the first paragraph.

By the end of the essay, the effective writer demonstrated the ability to succinctly summarize the literature, identify knowledge gaps, and propose a response to those gaps. In just two paragraphs, the writer shows the reviewers that she thinks in a linear fashion and can integrate information from diverse sources into a cogent statement. These skills are prerequisite to critically reviewing the literature and writing compelling capstone/dissertation proposals and are exactly what reviewers want to see.

Professional

It is vitally important that you present yourself in a professional manner. Graduate students are ambassadors for their program, and reviewers will look askance at your application if there are any concerns about your professionalism. First and foremost, be sure that your essay is free of spelling and grammatical errors. Do a spell and grammar check and then proofread the entire essay to ensure nothing was missed.

Second, read the directions carefully and provide only the information requested. Do not provide additional, unsolicited information. Third, actively strive to communicate a tone of professionalism. Find people who regularly review essays/personal statements (e.g., employers, admissions counselors, professors) and ask them to read your essay with an eye toward evaluating your professional demeanor. Do not attempt to be funny or profound, and avoid explicit spiritual/religious statements. These can cast you in an unprofessional light.

FIGURE 6.2

EFFECTIVE ESSAY EXAMPLE

I currently work with HIV-infected patients at an infectious diseases clinic located in a Health and Human Services Administration (HRSA)–designated medically underserved neighborhood. Due to the introduction of highly active antiretroviral therapy (HAART), AIDS-related mortality has plummeted. However, the aging of the HIV+ population has led to increased incidence of age-related morbidities, such as non-AIDS malignancies and cardiovascular disease (CVD), which were rarely seen in the pre-HAART era. Moreover, minorities, who represent 65% of persons living with HIV in the United States,[2,3] have a higher risk for health outcome disparities related to their infection, including CVD.[4,5]

In my practice, of which minorities comprise approximately 90% of the population, I see increasing numbers of HIV+ patients with significant coronary heart disease, leading to premature, yet preventable, deaths. Although statins can reduce the risk of CVD and related mortality, there are unique issues when they are administered to HIV+ persons. These issues include pharmacokinetic interactions with certain protease inhibitors, hepatotoxic effects that can be of

continues

continued

concern in the context of hepatitis C co-infection, and evidence of statin resistance among HIV+ patients who have metabolic syndrome.[6]

I am interested in investigating nonpharmacological therapies to produce durable reductions in CV risk factors in this vulnerable population. One promising option is supplementation with marine oils that are rich in omega-3 fatty acids. A large body of literature has demonstrated that marine oil-derived omega-3 fatty acids reduce atherosclerosis, stabilize plaques, decrease platelet aggregation, normalize dyslipidemic profiles, and reduce plasma concentrations of inflammatory cytokines, which are known to drive atherogenesis. However, to date, there are no published studies on the safety and efficacy of marine oil to favorably modulate CVD risk factors in HIV-infected persons.

My doctoral studies will represent the first step in a planned program of research to investigate the effects of marine oil as adjunctive therapy in the management of HIV infection. I have applied to X University because the faculty expertise is consonant with my research question. In particular, the work of Dr. Y in testing krill oil to reduce HIV-related inflammation and reverse immunosenescence is highly relevant to my proposed work.[7-12] My long-term goal is to function as an independent researcher who will lead interdisciplinary teams to investigate the effects of marine oil on HIV-related clinical outcomes.

FIGURE 6.3

INEFFECTIVE ESSAY EXAMPLE

I dreamed of being a nurse ever since I was a little girl. Thankfully, that dream came true. As I have gotten older my dreams have gotten bigger. Today I dream of being a nurse with a PhD! I know that I could accomplish many goals if I have the PhD credential.

My research interest is this: "how can we reduce cardiovascular disease risk in persons with HIV infection?" I work in an inner city HIV clinic and see firsthand how health disparities affect this population, including disparities related to heart disease. HIV-infected minorities are more likely to develop cardiovascular complications and die from them than HIV-infected Caucasians. I am passionate about complementary and alternative therapies and would like to study their affects on reducing cardiovascular risk factors and disease outcomes in medically-underserved HIV-infected persons. There are so many therapies that I'd love to investigate! These include meditation, yoga, therapeutic touch, and dietary supplements to name just a few. My head spins at the thought of the possibilities for research with this patient population! I see myself writing grants and leading research teams to answer these important questions! I see myself teaching the next generation of nurses to do research! If you would admit me to your program, you would make these dreams come true!

One Month Prior to Application Deadline

It is important that you are organized and follow the timeline that you have set for submission of all the components of the application to your targeted schools. You should submit the complete application 1 month or more prior to the deadline, including application forms, essay, resume, letters of recommendation, transcripts, and GRE scores, if required.

Call the admissions counselor to verify your application is received and complete.

Typically, admissions counselors review the applications and are willing to communicate missing documents.

The next step in the application process is a review of applications by program faculty leadership. This step involves a thorough review of each applicant's materials. Based on this evaluation, program faculty will select the applicants whom they will interview. As mentioned earlier, it is important that you are aware of the acceptance rates and competitiveness of specific programs. This will enable you to apply to programs that are a match to your background and credentials.

You will receive notification by the admissions counselors regarding the next step in the process: the interview. This notification will be either (1) information regarding how to schedule the interview or (2) a thank you for submission of the application; however, no interview will be scheduled.

IN REAL LIFE: BARBARA HINCH

I began my career as a professional nurse on a respiratory medicine unit at Rush Presbyterian-St. Lukes Medical Center. There was a clinical nurse specialist (CNS) on the unit who participated in rounds, helped staff with complex patients, led family meetings, conducted clinical research, and provided educational opportunities for the staff. This person became my role model and mentor for much of my career. Whenever I had a question about ventilator settings, medications, or anything related to my patient's care, I would turn to the CNS, who had a tremendous amount of knowledge to share with me. This inspired me to pursue graduate school, so that I could share my knowledge and expertise with other nurses. After finishing graduate school, I was able to teach about ventilators and caring for patients with respiratory issues to new critical care nurses, as well as graduate nursing students. I further pursued my graduate education by completing the acute care NP program several years later. Over the years, I have continued to meet with my mentor and have developed a strong relationship with her that will last a lifetime.

The Interview Process

The majority of graduate programs across the country require an interview as part of the application process. The interview serves several important purposes for the graduate program faculty:

- Determining whether your goals match the graduate program you are applying to

- Assessing your readiness for graduate school

- Determining whether your behavior, attitude, communication, and interpersonal dynamics reflect the professional nursing program, degree, and role you are pursuing.

The interview presents an opportunity for you to showcase your background, goals, and leadership potential. It is essential that you invest the time to prepare for this interview in order to position yourself well for a successful application process.

Preparing for the Interview

Thoroughly research the programs to which you are applying. The school's website will be useful in learning about its history, tradition, and culture. Become familiar with the program's faculty in relation to specialty areas, publications, and grants. Review the objectives, program of study, and degree requirements of your targeted program.

This research will help you to respond to interview questions. Also, it will help you develop relevant questions for the faculty interviewer. Following are potential questions that may be posed by MSN, DNP, and PhD program faculty and questions that you should be prepared to ask about the program.

Questions to Expect From MSN and DNP Program Interviewers

- What are your professional goals?
- What is your motivation to pursue graduate school now?
- Where do you see yourself professionally in 3 to 5 years?
- Describe your recent clinical experiences. How do they prepare you for this program?
- Why is our school of particular interest to you?
- What are your major strengths for completing this program?
- Describe experiences that reflect your leadership skills.
- Describe a challenging clinical situation you have dealt with recently. Why was it challenging, how was it resolved, and what did you learn from it?
- Describe a time where you were challenged to adapt to people from different backgrounds than your own. What did you do to resolve the situation?

Questions to Expect From PhD Program Interviewers

- Why do you want a PhD?
- What research topic interests you?
- What scholarly activities have you participated in (e.g., publications, presentations, peer review)?

- Describe your leadership experiences.

- What personal/professional resources and constraints will affect your pursuit of a PhD?

- What are your long-term goals?

Questions to Ask MSN and DNP Programs Interviewers

- What type(s) of clinical experiences do your students have?

- Who is responsible for identifying clinical preceptors?

- What is the role of the academic advisor?

- What are examples of capstone projects?

- What is the certification pass rate of this program?

- What main factors set your program apart from others?

- How does your school measure the success of its graduates?

- What percentage of your graduates attain positions in their chosen specialty?

Questions to Ask PhD Program Interviewers

- What is the average student:faculty ratio in the courses?

- How many PhD students does an advisor supervise?

- What is the success/attrition rate?

- What positions have program graduates assumed?

- What percentage of faculty has external funding?

- What funding/financial aid sources are available to students?

The Interview

Faculty interviewers are interested in what you have to say as well as how you present yourself (Christenbery, 2012). The following interview tips will be useful to review and consider as you prepare for your graduate school interviews:

- Make sure that you are 5 to 10 minutes early for the interview. This shows promptness and respect for other people's time.

- Select professional attire for the interview. For men, this would include a suit or dress pants, jacket, and tie. For women, a dress or suit would be appropriate.

- Body language is always important. Remain attentive to everything the interviewer is saying and maintain direct eye contact with him or her at all times.

- Try to be relaxed throughout the interview. Do not be afraid to engage in a little small talk if the interviewer takes the lead, especially at the beginning of the interview after you have first met.

- Always listen thoroughly first before responding to a question or comment. Respond thoughtfully to questions rather than blurting out responses. Taking a moment or two to briefly reflect on your responses demonstrates thoughtfulness and maturity.

- It is usually best to defer from asking several questions until the point at which the interviewer indicates that you now have the opportunity to do so. Many times, after the interviewer completes the process of describing aspects of the school and asking questions of you, he or she will ask something like: "Okay, now do you have any questions for me?" This is the time for you to ask those questions that you have prepared. However, it is acceptable to ask questions prior to this time, if the question relates directly to the subject being discussed during the flow of the interview.

Last Step in the Process

There will be a period of time following the interview before you hear about the admission decision. This period of time will vary from weeks to months, depending on the specific graduate program. Typically, the faculty interviewer will communicate this timeline to you during the interview. Also, this would be an appropriate question for you to ask at the end of the interview if it did not come up earlier.

This waiting period before receiving a decision may go on longer than expected. You can call or email the admissions counselor to inquire about this timeline. The culmination of the application process occurs with the formal communication of the admissions decision from the university. You will receive a formal notification of either (1) acceptance to the program or (2) denial of acceptance to the program.

Should you receive a denial of acceptance, do not be discouraged. As mentioned earlier, it is advisable to apply to more than one program. Also, targeting schools that match your experience and credentials is important. You can ask the admissions counselor for feedback on your application. You may be able to acquire advice on strengthening your application. This advice might include gaining more clinical experience in a specific area, retaking the GRE, or taking a graduate course as an unclassified student.

Conclusion

Graduate education will provide opportunities for a flexible career path and the rewards of career advancement. Now is the time to develop a plan to invest in your future career. Crafting successful applications requires your time, focus, and organizational skills. Table 6.2 presents an application checklist summarizing the key steps in the application process. This tool should help facilitate an organized and successful approach.

Table 6.2

Use the following checklist for applying to graduate school. Start this process at least 6 months before the admissions deadline.

DATE TO COMPLETE	CHECK WHEN COMPLETE	ACTIVITY
		Define your goals.
		Select target schools that have the program that is the best fit for you.
		Review the application requirements of each school.
		Develop a spreadsheet with admission dates and requirements for each school.
		Prepare for the GRE, if this is one of the requirements. Take the GRE and send the scores to the target schools.

DATE TO COMPLETE	CHECK WHEN COMPLETE	ACTIVITY
		Obtain original transcripts from all schools of record.
		Open application and begin entering data.
		Solicit references and request letters of recommendation.
		Write a compelling essay.
		Enter data on the application form, finalize your essay, and hit the "submit" button.
		Verify that your application is complete and received.
		Prepare for interview if invited.

References

Christenbery, T. L. (2012). Preparing BSN students for the doctor of nursing practice (DNP) application process: The faculty role. *Nurse Educator*, *37*(1), 30–35.

"CONTINUOUS EFFORT—NOT STRENGTH OR INTELLIGENCE—IS THE KEY TO UNLOCKING OUR POTENTIAL."

–WINSTON CHURCHILL

Chapter 7

Landing Fellowships and Internships

–Nancy Ridenour

AFTER READING THIS CHAPTER, YOU WILL BE ABLE TO:

- Understand how internships, residencies, and fellowships provide opportunities for career enhancement
- Communicate your strengths when seeking an internship, residency, or fellowship
- Understand the difference among a fellowship, residency, and internship
- Identify the knowledge and skills you gain from completing an internship, residency, or fellowship
- Prepare for your internship opportunities and strengthen your nursing portfolio
- Identify various internship and fellowship opportunities

Internships and Fellowships Help You Shine

The employment and professional world for RNs is changing rapidly. Changes in health care policies, technology, leadership styles, and generations are posing both challenges and opportunities. Employers are searching for employees who are self-starters and lifelong learners who utilize critical thinking skills and are quick to analyze and act on future trends in their profession. Nurses who show they can compete and earn highly competitive internships and fellowships distinguish themselves as motivated leaders. Employers take notice and hire these candidates over those that have taken a more traditional approach to employment.

RNs who are successful in moving up the career ladder develop multiple strategies in earning advanced degrees and certifications, as well as creating professional networks of influential health care leaders who assist them in finding lucrative employment.

What is an effective strategy that separates an RN professional from his or her peers in advancing in the nursing profession? A proven strategy that will assist your career, whether you are a student, RN professional, graduate student, faculty member, or administrator, is to apply for and receive internships and fellowships. Preparing your portfolio and strategically developing professional networks will enhance your competiveness for obtaining a prestigious fellowship or profession-enhancing internship.

IN REAL LIFE: NANCY RIDENOUR

There have been several pivotal moments in my career. I can recall each of these events in vivid detail regardless of how long ago they occurred. These key events chartered a course that provided experiences and accomplishments beyond what I had imagined. As I reflect on these momentous occasions, a common theme emerges: I was the beneficiary of the leadership vision of others.

The leadership development programs of the Robert Wood Johnson (RWJ) Foundation form the core of my professional growth and transformation. Very early in my career, I was selected as nurse practitioner faculty in the Primary Care Nurse Faculty Fellowship program, during which I worked with leading nursing faculty across the nation who developed expertise as nurse practitioners. I had the honor of working with Dr. Terrance Keenan. I became an RWJ Executive Nurse Fellow and learned the art of philanthropy, resulting in my work with the Sigma Theta Tau International Foundation. As a RWJ Health Policy Fellow, I had the profound experience of working on Ways and Means staff in the U.S. House of Representatives during the time that PPACA was written. Today I remain involved in the RWJ Action Coalitions, making the future of nursing report a reality. Throughout these fellowships, mentors provided support, challenged me to stretch my goals, and encouraged me to excel.

The lessons learned from my story: 1) Recognize and seek leadership opportunities, 2) apply leadership lessons to your current situation, and 3) pay forward by mentoring future leaders.

Internships and Fellowships

Internships are relatively short-term experiences that provide novice professionals with real world experience to enhance their professional skills. The internship is designed to provide mentored job skills to enhance the classroom experience. Often, faculty sponsors collaborate with the internship supervisor to enhance the learning environment. For example, a student may do an internship as part of his or her academic program. The faculty member coordinates with the internship preceptor to help the student meet course objectives. Internships can be part of the degree program or can be designed as the first 6 to 12 months of employment after graduating from the entry level nursing program and obtaining initial licensure. Some institutions use the term *residency* to describe the supervised period during the first 6 to 12 months of employment.

IN REAL LIFE:

Example of internship as part of academic program: *Robert is a graduating senior BSN nursing student at a state university. He has accepted a position at a university hospital in the adult ICU. Robert reports that he is prepared for the ICU because of the internship he completed during the summer term between his junior and senior*

continues

continued

year. He completed an unpaid 12-week internship at a tertiary care teaching hospital for academic credit. He was thrilled to be placed in a very busy emergency room but often felt overwhelmed by the pace and complexity of the work.

The clinical preceptor supervised all of his clinical work, and the nursing faculty member met with him on a regular basis to suggest additional resources, discuss learning challenges, and provide clarification of questions. Robert reports that these experiences increased his confidence and provided him with clinical skills that prepared him to accept the job in the ICU. His current employers recognized his expertise during the internship and were pleased to offer him the ICU position.

IN REAL LIFE:

Example of internship/residency as part of first job: *Pamela did not have the opportunity to do an internship as part of her academic program. She was, however, selected for the highly competitive paid nurse residency at a local hospital. The residency consisted of 1 year of practice with a clinical preceptor/mentor and formalized classroom work. She received entry level pay during the residency year. Successful completion of the residency will result in an automatic salary raise. Pamela describes the residency as increasing her skills and confidence in a supportive learning environment. She is now completing her residency and is prepared to handle a full patient load.*

The Future of Nursing: Leading Change, Advancing Health (Institute of Medicine, 2011) takes the internship/residency idea a step further by supporting the supervised residency as part of the initial transition from school to practice but also recommending that all nurses have a residency period when they are transitioning to a new clinical practice area. Margaret Flinter (2011), senior vice president and clinical director of the Community Health Center Inc. and founder of America's first nurse practitioner residency program, has developed a postmaster's or post-doctoral residency program for nurses who have recently completed a nurse practitioner program. As the recommendations from the future of nursing report are implemented, opportunities for internships and residencies will increase.

Whereas internships are most often intended for the novice professional, fellowships are designed to provide the more experienced professional with specific in-depth training and experience to further enhance his or her specialty expertise. Fellowships most often require master's or doctoral preparation.

What Will You Gain?

RNs who have had internships and fellowships can expect to learn in a short time about new trends and practices in:

- Health policy
- Leadership
- New trends, theories, and practices in research
- Business practices
- Management theory
- Skills and new techniques for their specialty area
- Curriculum development
- Teaching practices
- Information technology
- Finance and insurance
- Grant application and preparation
- Entrepreneurship
- Conflict resolution
- Forecasting future trends in health care

Whether you are a novice nurse or an experienced nurse seeking to increase your expertise, internships, residencies, and fellowships provide structured learning environments to enhance your career. The following table suggests milestones for you to consider when preparing your future career plans.

Table 7.1

Career Path Strategies

	INTERNSHIPS	FELLOWSHIPS	STRATEGY	BENEFITS
Prelicensure students	X		Students are more likely to get internships than fellowships.	Students are able to learn appropriate workforce habits and skills.
RNs in workforce	X	X	Trend is for more internship opportunities that are short-term.	It is a great opportunity to learn more about future trends in their specialty areas and learn new management skills.
MSNs, NPs		X	Goal is to learn more about research, policy trends, and clinical practices.	Fellowships are available that aid students in developing more robust research and clinical practices to enhance expertise.
PhD/DNP program		X	Doctoral students are provided mentoring and experiences that enhance research and/or clinical expertise.	The capacity to be mentored and perform guided research and/or specialty clinical practices enhances doctoral educational experience.
Postdoctoral		X	There is more extensive mentoring and capability to aggressively develop research programs and to enhance leadership skills and/or further clinical specialty expertise.	Individuals develop robust leadership, research, practice, and professional networks that make them highly employable.

	INTERNSHIPS	FELLOWSHIPS	STRATEGY	BENEFITS
Higher education faculty and administrators		X	Fellowships provide a focused opportunity to learn new teaching methods, research trends, gain leadership skills, and examine health care policy.	Fellowships provide opportunities to create new professional networks and learn skills from established professionals.
Nursing leaders		X	The opportunity to learn new management and policy changes is invaluable to chief nursing officers and leaders in health care.	Fellowships provide an opportunity to significantly increase professional networks in health care administration.

Pursuing Opportunities

Whether you are a novice nurse seeking your first internship or a seasoned professional looking for a career-enhancing fellowship, you will need to develop focused strategies to succeed. Creating a targeted resume developing relationships with key professionals and building your portfolio (as described in Chapter 3) are necessary steps to making sure your application stands out among the many.

You will be a step ahead of most other applicants if you present your materials in such a way to highlight your talents and show how your goals and expertise match the goals and outcomes expected by the sponsor. It may be necessary for you to relocate to take full advantage of an internship or fellowship.

Often internships are unpaid, and, although fellowships may provide a stipend, the amount of funding is often less than the salary of an experienced RN. Depending upon the focus of the program, you may be required to work full time on the internship or fellowship and give up outside employment during the period of the program. You must consider issues related to relocation, salary, and time commitment when deciding if an internship, residency, or fellowship is for you.

Winning Strategies for Success

Successful strategies for obtaining competitive internships, residencies, and fellowships include knowing and communicating your strengths. How can you show that you can offer a solution to some of the problems facing your future employer? How will your unique skills and expertise be helpful to the organization sponsoring the position you are seeking?

Networking: As a student, it is important to get to know your instructors. They can provide invaluable assistance in identifying future opportunities and supporting your application. As a seasoned nurse, it is useful for you to meet key leaders in your field. All nurses should seek to meet the leaders of the professional organizations that support their interests. For example, joining the National Student Nurses' Association or the American Nurses Association is a good start. Meeting the local, state, and national officers and volunteering for committee work will introduce you to people in leadership positions and provide future opportunities. Social networking can be helpful as well. You need to be aware, however, of the downside of social networking. Future employers and search committees will search the Internet for information about applicants. Make sure that your Internet presence reflects what you want to convey about yourself as a professional.

Resume: Think of your resume as a way to market your special talents. Your resume should be tailored to the specific aims and goals of the program to which you are applying. This is not a one-size-fits-all situation! In order to be competitive and to put your best foot forward, your resume should highlight how you can enhance the work of the sponsor while you are achieving your own learning goals.

Many resumes consist of a chronological list of accomplishments. Although this information is important, it is vital that you present your information in a manner that brings attention to your accomplishments. Think of what you are most proud of about your work. What accomplishments describe your abilities? Write your resume with action and outcomes in mind. Keep technical jargon to a minimum unless specifically requested in the application materials. For example, compare the two entries below. Which applicant would you be more interested in interviewing?

Applicant A: 2011-2012: President of local chapter of Sigma Theta Tau International

Applicant B: 2011-2012: While president of local chapter of Sigma Theta Tau International, increased funding for research scholarships by 30%

Most readers will agree that Applicant B tells us more about the abilities and accomplishments of the candidate. Take a look at your resume and add action to your chronological list. As you review the application materials for the program you are interested in, make sure you highlight your skills, accomplishments, and interests with those described in the application materials.

Feedback: When you complete your first draft of your targeted resume, it is helpful to seek feedback. Ask a friend or family member to suggest areas where you might further highlight your accomplishments. A professor or co-worker who knows your work can provide feedback, as well. If possible, ask your professor or coworker to suggest someone who can provide an unbiased review of your work. Ask the person who does not know you to provide feedback in the following areas:

- What type of internship/fellowship fits the interests and skills described in your resume?

- What strengths are described in your resume?

- What suggestion can they provide to improve the resume?

Letters of Reference: As you read in Chapter 5, if the application requires letters of reference, you will need to identify people who can speak to your work and address the specific areas requested in the application. Because this is a process that requires your reference to respond to your application, you need to start communicating with potential references early in the process. It is critical that you seek permission of the person whom you are considering as a potential reference. You need to have a conversation with the person to describe your interests, talents, and how you are an excellent candidate for the position. Make sure that the person is willing and able to provide required reference materials in the designated time frame.

In addition to providing your resume to the person serving as a reference for your application, it is helpful to include a list of personal objectives along with a personal statement regarding your interests and accomplishments that match those of the position you are seeking. The person serving as your reference can use these materials to craft a solid letter of support. Under no circumstances should you provide a name of a reference without first obtaining permission from the proposed reference.

Letter of Application: If the application requires a cover letter, make sure that you specifically address the items mentioned in the application materials. The letter should address the future employer's needs, not yours. For example, address the following topics:

- Compelling reasons why you are a good fit for the organization

- How your talents are a good fit for the organization

- How your education, skills, and expertise can be beneficial to the organization

The letter should address specifics of the organization, the position, and how you will enhance the work of the organization.

Appearance of the Application: If the application is done online, it is likely the materials will be reviewed for keywords. Make sure that your application letter and resume speak directly to the characteristics and criteria delineated in the application materials. The resume and the letter need to be professional and without errors. Never underestimate the power of the visual impact of your materials. The layout should be easy to read and have the appearance of a professional document. Do not try to compress too much information in a small space. If the application has a word, page, or character limit, make sure you do not exceed the specified limits! Remember, use of white space and margins can make the difference in how much attention your application receives. Ask yourself and your reviewers the following questions:

- Is it clear and concise?

- Does it tell my story?

- Is it visually attractive?

- Does it convey action and accomplishment?

- Is it targeted and relevant to the position being sought?

The most important question of all: Will the resume and letter of application lead to an invitation to interview?

Preparing for the Interview

Once you secure an interview, it is time to shine. Preparing for the interview can be the margin of difference that gets you the position in the midst of extreme competition. Preparation includes several phases:

- Learn all you can about the organization: its mission and values; its organizational structure; its leadership. More specifically, learn about the people who will be interviewing you. What is their position in the organization? What are their accomplishments? This preparation will help you understand the employer's perspective and decrease the potential for interview questions you have not anticipated.

- Talk with people who have been successful in obtaining the internship, residency, or fellowship you are seeking. They are interested in helping applicants succeed and can provide you with helpful hints regarding the interview process.

- Practice responding to general questions like, "Why are you seeking this position?"; "Tell me about yourself."; "What strengths do you bring to the positions?"; or "What areas of weakness do you need to improve?" When discussing your weakness, be sure to indicate how you are working to improve and turn your weakness into a strength.

- Dress for success: When deciding what to wear for the interview, err on the side of business conservative. It is best not to wear cologne or perfume. It is helpful to practice interviewing in the clothes and shoes you plan to wear. Practice sitting up straight in the chair with your feet flat on the floor.

- Being secure but not overconfident in the interview is important. Coming prepared will help alleviate your anxiety. If you are asked an unexpected question, or are not sure how you should respond to a question, ask the interviewer for clarification.

- Actively listen to the questions and respond succinctly. As a rule of thumb, your response should not be more than 2 minutes. If you can imbed your response in a story, you are more likely to engage your audience. Practice short stories about your accomplishments that describe a situation, highlight the actions you took to address the situation, and summarize the results you achieved.

- Attach data and outcomes to your results, if possible.

- Prepare in advance a few questions you would like to ask the interviewers.

- Many fellowships/internships will publish a timeline of when participants will be notified of the outcome of the interviews. If you do not find this information, you should ask when decisions will be made and how you will learn the results. Clarify who is the person you should contact after the interview and the best way to reach him or her.

- Thank all the participants for their time and interest.

What Can You Expect After the Interview?

Review the information in the application materials or during the interview to determine how long you should expect to wait and whether you will be notified by mail, email, or telephone. Remember during the application process to provide your current contact information so you can be reached in a timely manner. If you do not hear anything after the stated deadline, wait a few days and get in touch with the designated contact person. Do not assume silence means you have not been accepted. And, regardless of whether you are selected, thank the participants for the opportunity.

What to Do if You Are Not Selected

Notification that you have not been chosen can be difficult. Make sure you maintain a cordial and professional demeanor in all communications. Unless the materials you have received specify that feedback will not be provided, you should prepare questions to ask the contact person for feedback to help you improve your performance in the future. Consider this feedback carefully and incorporate suggestions in future applications. Many internships and fellowships will consider a second application. Clarify with the contact person if the specific opportunity you sought will consider future applications.

Congratulations! You've Been Accepted

Continue to maintain a professional demeanor when discussing the details of the fellowship or internship you have landed. Make sure that you obtain details about the logistics of your new position. For example, you may be asked to relocate, prepare documents before starting, and complete specified readings. In addition, you should clarify details regarding start and end dates, dress codes, and performance expectations prior to beginning your fellowship or internship.

Then you can begin to prepare for potentially one of the most meaningful experiences along your career journey.

Resources for Internships

Many health care facilities offer internships to undergraduate students during their last year of their pre-licensure program or immediately upon graduation and passing NCLEX. Check with institutions you are interested in working for after graduation to see what internship opportunities are available.

You should begin thinking about these opportunities during your first or second semester of the nursing program. You need to understand requirements so you can plan your educational program to make sure you meet requirements for future internships. Talking with the clinical nurses you work with during your clinical rotations can help you to understand available opportunities.

Residency opportunities for nurses transitioning to a new clinical area are being developed in response to the future of nursing report (Institute of Medicine, 2011). Check with your employer and graduate program for residency opportunities.

Several professional organizations offer internships.

- The American Public Health Association (APHA), for example, has several internships and fellowships: www.apha.org/about/careers/internships

- Sigma Theta Tau International (STTI) lists many volunteer opportunities for nurses to increase their leadership and clinical expertise: www.nursingsociety.org/VolunteerConnect/VolunteeringHC/Pages/cmap_volunteer.aspx

- The Centers for Disease Control and Prevention (CDC) offers internships for undergraduate or graduate students still in school and for health professionals who are in training: www.cdc.gov/Fellowships/StudentInternships.html

- The following site also lists available internships: www.nurseresidencyprograms.com

Resources for Fellowships

Because fellowships are most often designed for established professionals, they are less numerous than internship opportunities. By their nature, fellowships require specialization. Just as described for internships, it is important to plan ahead regarding fellowship applications. You will need to strategically plan the timing of your application and line up your references well in advance to make sure you are competitive.

Two well-known fellowships are from the Robert Wood Johnson Foundation: The Executive Nurse Fellowship (ENF) and the Health Policy Fellowship.

The Executive Nurse Fellowship (ENF) is a 3-year fellowship for nurses in senior executive roles from fields such as public or community health, science and research, corporate health, academia, government, and military health service. Fellows remain in their current positions as they receive training and mentoring. Each fellow designs and implements a leadership project with his or her employer to lead their institution through policy or procedural changes. Leadership development sessions that touch on 20 different competency areas, action learning, executive coaching, and mentoring opportunities add up to a life-changing experience that has an impact not only on the fellows but on their institution and colleagues: www.executivenursefellows.org

Health Policy Fellowship: This fellowship, housed at the National Academy of Science at the Institute of Medicine in Washington, DC, provides midcareer health professionals and behavioral and social scientists a 1-year residency working directly on health policy at the federal level. A 3-month orientation is followed by full-time work with legislators and their staff. Fellows receive leadership coaching, media training, site visits, and networking opportunities with some of the most important health policymakers of our time. The program instills in fellows a deep understanding of the role of government—and government policy—in the health of all Americans: www.healthpolicyfellows. org/home.php

The World Health Organization (WHO) offers several unpaid opportunities. Although called internships, the competitive applicant is most likely an experienced health professional: www. who.int/employment/internship/en

The Centers for Disease Control and Prevention (CDC) offers career training fellowships for those who have a graduate degree: www.cdc.gov/Fellowships/CareerInternships.html

Nontraditional Resources for Fellowships and Internships

The World Health Organization and the United Nations offer several opportunities for recent graduates in the JPO Program (Junior Professional Officer). The program is supported by member organizations, and it is necessary to determine if your country is supporting a position: www.jposc.org

WHO also has a special program in the Nursing and Midwifery Office for nurse or midwife leaders to participate in development of health policy and normative tools and models of nursing and midwifery at the global level: www. who.int/hrh/nursing_midwifery/internships/en/index.html

Harvard School of Public Health offers a Program on Health Care Negotiation and Conflict Resolution: www.hsph.harvard.edu/research/hcncr

IOM Scholar-in-Residence: A yearlong immersion in health policy at the Institute of Medicine, supported by the American Academy of Nursing, the American Nurses Association, and the American Nurses Foundation. www. aannet.org/iom-scholar-in-residence

The Health Services Research Information Center (HSRIC) of the National Library of Medicine catalogs several fellowships available in areas ranging from patient safety and comparative effectiveness research to health policy: www.nlm.nih.gov/hsrinfo/grantsites.html

AACN-Wharton Executive Leadership Program: American Association of Colleges of Nursing and the University of Pennsylvania's Wharton School of Business offer a 4-day program that presents relevant, timely content designed to advance cheif academic administrators to a higher level of leadership. www. aacn.nche.edu/leading-initiatives/aacn-wharton-executive-leadership-program

AACN Leadership for Academic Nursing Program: "AACN sponsors an executive leadership fellowship tailored specifically for aspiring and new deans. Designed to prepare a more diverse, younger pool of leaders for nursing programs, this professional development experience encompasses an assessment and evaluation of leadership skills, opportunities for strategic networking and case study development, consultation to achieve long-term goals, and identification of key partnerships." www.aacn.nche.edu/membership/networks/lanp

Programs exist for nurses who wish to increase their understanding of health care advocacy. Several organizations sponsor short-term educational programs accompanied with legislative visits.

- NIWI: Nurses in Washington Internship: The Nursing Organizations Alliance sponsors a 3-day intensive orientation to the legislative process culminating in visits to legislators. www.nursing-alliance.org/content.cfm/id/niwi

- Student Policy Summit: Sponsored by American Association of Colleges of Nursing, a 3-day intensive for undergraduate and graduate students with didactic content and Hill visits. www.aacn.nche.edu/government-affairs/student-policy-summit

References

Flinter, M. (2011). From new nurse practitioner to primary care provider: Bridging the transition through FQHC-based residency training. *OJIN: The Online Journal of Issues in Nursing, 17*(1). Retrieved from http://www.nursingworld.org/MainMenuCategories/ANAMarketplace/ANAPeriodicals/OJIN/TableofContents/Vol-17-2012/No1-Jan-2012/Articles-Previous-Topics/From-New-Nurse-Practitioner-to-Primary-Care-Provider.html

Institute of Medicine. (2011). *The future of nursing: Leading change, advancing health*. Washington, DC: National Academies Press.

"Don't raise your voice; improve your argument."

–Archbishop Desmond Tutu

Chapter 8

Expressing Your Professional Best

–Anne E. Belcher

AFTER READING THIS CHAPTER, YOU WILL BE ABLE TO:

- Recognize the importance of effective communication in nursing
- Utilize tools to effectively listen and improve communication
- Choose tactics from various persuasion theories to enhance your communication with others
- Pay attention to your own (as well as others') nonverbal communication
- Understand impact of social networking on communication
- Utilize appreciative inquiry technique to help frame discussions based on what is working well
- Carefully plan persuasive presentations for maximum impact

Persuasive Communication Requires Planning, Understanding, and Self-Awareness

---

IN REAL LIFE: ANNE BELCHER

As a newly master's-prepared nurse, I accepted a teaching position at The Florida State University. How exciting to teach baccalaureate nursing students in the classroom and in the clinical setting! The more experience I gained as a teacher, the more I wanted to learn so that I could be an even better teacher.

I decided to enroll in a course on adult learning at the College of Education, knowing that the students with whom I was working, as well as most of the patients for whom we cared, needed to be appreciated as different from younger learners. Imagine my surprise and delight when I learned about Malcolm Knowles and andragogy and began to incorporate his principles of adult learning into my lectures and clinical experiences.

This course was so meaningful that I decided to enroll in another course. As you may now anticipate, I enrolled in the next course and the next, until the chair of the Department of Higher Education called me in and said that if I wanted to continue to take courses, I must apply for admission to the doctoral program.

This was indeed a turning point in my nursing career, because I perceived that I was making the decision to become a nurse educator. I decided that the rewards of teaching were so significant that I wanted to be "the best that I could be." So I applied to and was accepted into the PhD program in higher education/adult education and now, 40 years later, I am reminded by my students every day that I indeed made the right decision.

In today's world, everyone is being bombarded with information from numerous sources, including face-to-face conversations with individuals and groups, television, radio, newspapers, the Internet, and social media. This is also happening in health care—to you as a health care provider, to patients and families, and to organizations and communities. Not only are you challenged by the volume and sources of information, but also by whether it is valid, accurate, and timely. So how do you manage this tremendous influx of information so that you can respond to and use it effectively in your professional life? And how do you in turn express your messages and share your information in a clear, concise, and persuasive manner that reaches your target audience(s)?

Communication has always been an important part of nursing. In nursing school, you learned about therapeutic communication and the differences among sympathy, empathy, and rapport. I remember struggling with those differences and their value in my communication with patients, families, classmates, and faculty. I continue to ponder those differences and what seem to be the changing rules about communication, especially with the advent of Facebook, Twitter, and other social media affecting how people communicate.

Lisa Kennedy Sheldon, an advanced practice nurse at St. Joseph Hospital in New Hampshire; Rosann Barrett, a faculty member at Regis College in Weston, Massachusetts; and Lee Ellington, a faculty member at the University of Utah, noted in their article that "the exchange of information, feelings, and concerns is of vital importance in therapeutic relationships in health care" (Sheldon, Barrett, & Ellington, 2006, p. 141-147). Their observation holds true in any relationship and in any type of communication. Communicating well is a skill that can be learned. For meaningful persuasive communication, the nurse needs to organize, send, and receive information required for effective decision-making.

Although high-technology interventions are gaining popularity in nursing and in society, clear communication requires three components: listening, reflecting back, and clarifying information (Garofalo & Murphy, 2014). According to Beth Boynton (2009), an organizational development consultant and author of the book *Confident Voices: The Nurses' Guide to Improving Communication and Creating Positive Workplaces,* communication not only involves a message between a sender and a receiver but also can be influenced by such variables as power dynamics, clinical urgency, personalities, conflict, time limitations, and fatigue. Being aware of and sensitive to these variables can impact persuasive communication.

For example, acknowledging a power differential between you and the individual or group with whom you are working can relieve tension that may exist. Your audience, for example, the staff on a unit where you are the clinical nurse specialist (CNS), may need to be assured that you are working with them as a colleague and that their "buy-in" to your ideas or recommendations is important. So you are eager to answer their questions and address their concerns before a decision is made.

GOOD TO KNOW:

For those people who are uncomfortable speaking in public, Toastmasters can be an effective way to overcome the jitters. Find a Toastmaster near you at www.toastmasters.org.

If you are the staff nurse on the low end of the totem pole, you need to acknowledge the experience and position of those CNSs and managers above you and share your ideas as derived from your observations in the practice setting, literature review, and consultation with nurse leaders.

The issue of time requires that you be well organized, well prepared, and succinct in your presentation. Brevity is a valued commodity, especially to the listeners. You might provide the individual or group with handouts to view prior to and/or during the discussion so that you can focus on the decision to be made and not spend excessive amounts of time on the background of the issue.

This approach is also helpful when your audience is tired, either from working prior to the discussion or because of stressors in the workplace. As you know, fatigue can adversely affect your attention span and patience. Acknowledging these factors in your listeners often gains their attention and heightens their willingness to listen to your presentation.

Good Listening Skills Cannot Be Overemphasized

It is always difficult to listen to another person speak, as you are often already formulating your answer to the question or thinking about your next question or comment. Boynton developed the GRRRR for great listening model, which provides you with a structured approach to listening. It focuses on how the message is received more so than how it is delivered (Boynton, 2009). Here are its components:

- Greeting: Begin with "hello" and the use of the other person's name.

- Respectful listening: Let the other person finish sentences without interruption, but do make occasional acknowledgements such as "yes," "okay," or "hmmm." Make eye contact, nod, and use other "receptive" body language.

- Review (also called validating): Summarize the information being conveyed to indicate that you understand the message correctly and to give the speaker the opportunity to correct any misunderstanding; this also allows you to clarify your concerns and express other thoughts without being intimidating. This can be challenging because it requires that the listeners separate their perspective and response from those of the speaker, which can be influenced by such variables as time, stress, tradition, skill, training, mood, and even the weather.

- Recommend or request more information: You should now have enough information to make recommendations or to request more information.

- Reward: You might say, "Thank you," or "I appreciate your comments"; invite further conversation by saying, "Call me if you need to..."

Practice these skills when you next speak with a colleague about an issue on which you may not agree. I have done so and found that I did listen better and was able to reach consensus with another nurse on an issue about which we both were passionate!

Theories of Persuasion

Persuasion has been defined as "human communication that is designed to influence others by modifying their beliefs, values, or attitudes" (Simons, 1976, p. 21). Requirements to be met in order for the sender and the recipient to consider a message persuasive have been described in literature (O'Keefe, 1990): There is a goal and intent to achieve that goal on the part of the messenger; communication is the means to achieve that goal, and the recipient must have free will. Thus persuasion is not accidental or coercive.

Social judgment theory suggests that knowing a person's attitude on various topics can provide you with clues about how to approach someone persuasively. You already know—but might not always think—to validate someone's feeling before providing your message. For example, the issue of mandatory flu shots causes some nurses to resist. Until you understand the reason(s) for their attitude, you will not be able to persuade them to participate in the flu shot campaign. Though you may know that "it is the right thing to do," you need to appreciate an individual's past experiences, fears, and concerns about autonomy.

People make judgments about the content of messages based on their anchors (stance) and attitudes: the latitude of acceptance, the latitude of rejection, and the latitude of noncommitment (Sherif, Kelly, Rodgers, Sarup, & Tittler, 1973). Your reaction to a persuasive message depends on your position on the topic. You could develop a Likert scale that has a list of statements to which your audience either agrees or disagrees. The resultant map is a function of how ego-involved that person is about that topic. Thus, people make judgments about messages based on their preexisting attitudes. If you wish to persuade an individual or a group to accept your recommendations, you will need to determine their attitudes about the subject and to present your argument with the lowest latitude of rejection possible.

True persuasion can only occur if the message you send is in the receiver's (1) latitude of noncommitment or (2) at the edges of the latitude of acceptance. Create a Likert scale, with the anchors being statements about the topic with which you ask your colleagues, patients, or family to agree or disagree. The results/scores will give you the basis for planning further discussion and presentation of information that may be persuasive.

Another way of looking at persuasion is to view the group as your audience and to determine their values, beliefs, and attitudes before you create your message. A great example is trying to persuade colleagues with an associate degree in nursing to pursue a baccalaureate degree. There is certainly an emotional component to nurses' reaction to this message, but there is also factual information that may be persuasive (for example, the need to have a BS in nursing in order to be hired into/retained in a Magnet hospital).

The elaboration likelihood model (ELM) views persuasion as a cognitive event, meaning that individuals use mental processes of motivation and reasoning (or a lack thereof) to accept or reject a persuasive message. This model, developed by Richard E. Petty and John Cacioppo (1986), emphasizes the importance of understanding audience members before creating a persuasive message. The authors suggest two possible routes of influence: centrally routed messages and peripherally routed messages.

Centrally routed messages include a wealth of information, rational arguments, and evidence to support a particular position. These messages are more likely to create long-term changes for the recipient when that individual is highly motivated to process all of the information provided, and the individual must be able to process the message cognitively. Elaborate arguments have to reflect the audience's reaction to the quality and arrangement of the arguments you present:

- Strong arguments create a positive cognitive response, inoculate the listeners against counter-persuasion, and are more likely to create long-term change in attitude, which leads to predictable behavior.

- Neutral arguments generate a noncommittal response from the audience, with no change in attitude.

- Weak arguments produce a negative cognitive response, possibly resulting in reinforcement of the opposing point of view.

When motivation or ability is missing from the audience, for example, nurses who have held associate degrees for many years, you might try the peripheral route to persuasion. These messages rely on the listener's emotional involvement and persuasion through more superficial, quick-and-easy ways to produce results. Such arguments, such as increased income, eligibility for promotion, and possible higher-level leadership roles, might apply to this audience emotionally. However, the change that occurs is short-term, if there is change at all. The common cues that signal the use of a peripheral message are:

- Authority (often used by leaders, supervisors, and parents): Although the nurses may want to please you because of your status and "power," they may come to resent your use of these factors.

- Commitment (based on one's dedication to a product, social cause, group affiliation, etc.): Appealing to the nurses' love of profession, their team, or the organization may be persuasive.

- Liking (stresses affinity toward a person, place, or object; if you like me/my colleagues/my organization, you will like my message): More of a personal appeal based on friendship or social affiliation.

- Reciprocity (emphasize a give-and-take relationship): For example, "If you enroll in a BS program, I will consider you for the next vacancy on an influential committee or a different shift."

- Scarcity (preys on the listener's worry of missing out on something): For example, "If you do not pursue the degree, you will be left behind by your colleagues with regard to opportunities for advancement and professional service."

- Social proof (use of peer pressure): Can persuade some nurses to pursue the BS because they will be in classes with their friends and will have the support of their peers for academic work.

As with centrally routed arguments, peripheral messages can be evaluated as positive, neutral, or negative. Persuasion is more than the result of providing others with new or refined beliefs. Instead, influence is viewed as an intrapersonal event, which occurs when incongruence between your attitudes and behavior creates a tension that is relieved either by altering your beliefs or your behaviors. Leon Festinger (1962), who created the cognitive dissonance theory (CDT), postulated that when you are presented with information that is inconsistent with what you believe, you experience an imbalance or dissonance. This dissonance becomes a very persuasive tool because you feel so uneasy with contradictory beliefs and actions that you try to minimize the discomfort. There are three possible relationships between beliefs and behaviors:

- Irrelevance: Beliefs and behaviors that have nothing to do with each other

- Consonance: Two pieces of information are in balance or achieve congruence

- Dissonance: Two pieces of information contradict each other

For example, if you are trying to persuade your nursing colleagues to stop smoking, you may have to acknowledge that the nurses may see their beliefs about the dangers of smoking and their behavior of still smoking as being mutually exclusive. You need to avoid dissonance by not focusing on the number of persons who smoke and never get sick. Instead, you need to provide data that indicates the adverse results of smoking, which would be indicative of balance/consonance.

There is a magnitude of dissonance; some forms of dissonance produce greater discomfort than others. Three variables impact the magnitude of dissonance:

- Perceived importance: How important is the nurse's health to her/him?

- Dissonance ratio (proportion of incongruent beliefs held in relation to the number of consonant beliefs): How many reasons does the nurse articulate for smoking in relation to knowledge of the adverse results of smoking?

- Your ability to rationalize, or justify, the dissonance: Many nurses are quite skilled at explaining the contradictions, even though the evidence does not support their explanations.

The processes of selective exposure, attention, interpretation, and retention can be used to minimize dissonance:

- Selective exposure—one actively avoiding information that is inconsistent with previously established beliefs or behaviors—of course, this helps the smoking nurse deal with the dissonance but does not reduce the health risks.

- Selective attention—if you have to expose yourself to a situation that is incongruent with your beliefs, you will only pay attention to information that reaffirms your beliefs—again, this helps the nurse to cope with the voluminous health information to which he/she is exposed.

- Selective interpretation—you will carefully decipher ambiguous information so that you can perceive it as consistent with your beliefs—it may be a challenge, but many individuals are successful in doing so.

- Selective retention—you retain information that upholds your viewpoint while dismissing or forgetting information that creates dissonance—an interesting coping strategy that you probably use effectively in a wide variety of situations.

Consider the value of understanding cognitive dissonance when you are working with patients and families whose diagnoses require a fairly dramatic change in lifestyle. CDT will help you to understand their possible resistance to what you are trying to teach them, information that you know is evidence-based and essential to their coping with the illness! CDT should also help you to address their resistance to needed changes in behavior.

Nonverbal Communication

While persons listen to what you say and the inflection you use, they also are looking at your nonverbal communication. All your nonverbal behaviors—the gestures you use, the way you sit or stand, how fast you talk, how loudly you talk, how close you stand to your listener(s), how much eye contact you have—often sends messages that enhance or contradict what you are saying. Even silence is a form of nonverbal communication. When faced with mixed messages, the listener has to choose whether to give credence to your verbal or nonverbal message. There is evidence to indicate that the listener will choose the nonverbal communication because it is an unconscious, natural language known to show your true feelings and intentions in any given moment.

For example, you are talking with a patient about his need to reduce the salt in his diet, including the probable elimination of favorite foods such as hot dogs and French fries; he is looking at you and nodding, but his arms are crossed and he moves farther from you the longer you talk. Or, you are teaching a group of nurses a "mandatory" skill, and they are in their seats but frequently checking their cell phones, talking to one another, and yawning. These are fairly obvious examples of negative nonverbal communication; the signs might be more subtle, as some persons can give the impression of listening and agreeing, but in reality, they are "tuned out" and disagreeing with what you are saying.

In order to be an effective and persuasive communicator, it is important to be sensitive not only to the body language of others, but also to your own. According to Edward Wertheim (1988), author of *The Importance of Effective Communication*, nonverbal communication cues can play five roles:

Repetition (repeating the verbal message): The nonverbal activity may reflect the message; for example, if you tell the patient to exercise, the patient may run in place as a way of demonstrating his understanding of what you are saying.

Contradiction (contradicting a message the person is trying to convey): When you are showing energy in your voice and comments, the listener may roll his eyes or yawn.

Substitution (substituting for a verbal message): For example, your eyes can often convey more than your words do. You may open your eyes wide as a way to emphasize the importance of your comment.

Complementing (adding to a verbal message, such as praise complemented with a pat on the back): Often the nonverbal signal or sign reinforces the message; for example, you tell a staff colleague that she handled a patient emergency well and give her a hug or squeeze her hand or arm.

Accenting (underlining a verbal message, such as using hand gestures): Using your hands to emphasize what you are saying, for example, by knocking on the table, pointing to the board or slide, or waving one or both hands in a certain direction.

There are numerous types of nonverbal communication of which you should be aware and use to be congruent with your verbal communication, including facial expressions, body movements and posture, gestures, eye contact, touch, space, and voice. It is difficult, if not impossible, to control all of the signals you send about what you are thinking and feeling. It is important to stay focused on what you are saying and to be sure your words match your nonverbal communication. It is also important to listen carefully and to observe the nonverbal communication of your audience (Segal, Smith, Boose, & Jaffe, 2013).

Social Networking

Social network sites, such as Facebook, Twitter, and blogs, are online communities where individuals and groups can meet, interact, and exchange information. As you know, there are hundreds of web tools available to use for networking, collaborating, and information seeking and communicating.

These sites and tools can be valuable to you in persuasive communication, especially if you wish to reach large groups or people who are geographically diverse. There is an art to writing for these sites, as the clarity of your words will definitely affect the response of the readers. Photographs, diagrams, YouTube links, podcasts, and other illustrative media can positively impact the persuasiveness of your presentation.

It is useful to have individuals similar to those in your intended audience review your presentation before you send it; often what seems clear, concise, and relevant to you is not perceived that way by those with whom you are communicating. An excellent resource for you has recently been published by Sigma Theta Tau International: The author is Robert Fraser, and the book is titled *The Nurse's Social Media Advantage: How Making Connections and Sharing Ideas Can Enhance Your Nursing Practice.*

Appreciative Inquiry

An intriguing approach to communication is offered by the creators of Appreciative Inquiry. David Cooperrider and his associates at Case Western Reserve University (Srivastva & Cooperrider, 1990) introduced the term, which suggests that you look for what is working in a group or organization and build on those successes. The "tangible result of the inquiry process is a series of statements that describe where the organization wants to be, based on the high moments of where they have been. Because the statements are grounded in real experience and history, people know how to repeat their success" (Hammond, 1998, p. 7). What an exciting idea for you to use in persuasive communication.

An example from Sue Annis Hammond, an expert in Appreciative Inquiry, is applicable to our work with patients, families, and colleagues: Ask the group with whom you are meeting to share examples of what it feels like and what it looks like to be treated with dignity and respect. The group will probably be able to identify the circumstances that make dignity and respect possible and share statements that reflect common themes. The result: Instead of a list of "don'ts," the group members are inspired to re-create those positive circumstances as often as possible.

So, for example, if you find yourself presenting a change in policy, procedure, or organization to your clients, classmates, colleagues, or the faculty, begin with asking them what is working well and how those positive aspects can be retained. Then discuss those less-than-positive aspects and what can be enhanced or added to the situation to make those aspects more positive.

Hammond (1998) offers some sample questions with which to begin Appreciative Inquiry:

- Describe a time when you felt the group performed really well. What were the circumstances during that time?

- Describe a time when you were proud to be a member of the group. Why were you proud?

- What do you value most about being a member of this group? Why?

As you can readily see, these are useful questions to ask yourself about groups of which you are a member, so that you too can be persuasive in your communication with that group.

Persuasive Presentations to Groups

With regard to presentations (podium, classroom, clinical setting), Hinton (personal communication, January 30, 2013) wrote that you should have the attitude that:

- You are inspiring the members of the audience with your presentation

- You are teaching something to the members of the audience with your presentation

- You are persuading the members of the audience that your presentation is significant

Find a quiet pace to draft your presentation and focus only on this task by asking the following questions:

- What is the basic purpose of your talk?

- Who is the audience?

- What does the audience expect of you?

- What visual medium is the most appropriate?

- How much time do you have?

- What is your story? People like to hear stories, and they help the audience remember your presentation.

- If you want to convey one message, what would that be? In other words, if you want the audience to remember one thing, what would that be?

- How can you show empathy for your audience?

- How can you inspire, teach, and persuade?

When giving a persuasive speech or presentation, it is also important for you to remember to:

- Use simple eye contact

- Change your presentation as you watch the reactions of your audience

- Inject some humor; be sure it is natural and not forced

- Show your passion

- Show your appreciation for the audience

- Practice, practice, practice

- Use a conversational style

- Remember that audiences are very forgiving if you make a mistake

Hinton is a professor in the Department of Cell Biology in the School of Medicine at the University of Virginia. He conducts workshops on presentations and shared the work of his colleagues (Nancy Duarte, Daniel Pink, and Garr Reynolds) with me when I contacted him.

Schwartz, Dowell, Aperi, & Kalet (2007) developed 10 guidelines to increase your efficiency in assessing the validity and results of a study and increase your confidence in providing the core essentials of a presentation. Their guidelines are as follows:

- Describe the case or problem that attracted you to this paper.

- Explain how you came across this article.

- Describe the study.

- Describe the research question.

- State the importance, relevance, and context of the question.

- Describe the methods by giving more detail on the components of the question.

- State your answers to the critical appraisal questions on validity.

- Summarize the primary results.
- Describe why you think the results can or cannot be applied to your patients/situation.
- Conclude with your own decision about the utility of the study in your practice—resolve the case or question with which you began.
- Prepare a one-page summary of the outline above as a handout.

Schwartz and his colleagues found that these guidelines have "dramatically improved the enthusiasm for, quality of, and attendance at our journal clubs" (A-9).

Persuasive communication helps you to express your professional best through both verbal and nonverbal interaction with colleagues, patients, and families. The strategies discussed are applicable to face-to-face conversations and presentations. Enjoy learning about, practicing, and enacting those aspects of communication that will help you to express your professional best now and always!

References

Boynton, B. (2009). How to improve your listening skills. *American Nurse Today, 4*(9), 50-51.

Festinger, L. (1962). *A theory of cognitive dissonance.* Stanford, CA: Stanford University Press.

Garofalo, P. F., & Murphy, D. J. (2014). Clear communication and information management in the community. In Holzemer, S. P., & Klainberg, M. (Eds.), *Community health nursing: An alliance for health* (pp. 103-119). Burlington, MA: Jones Bartlett.

Hammond, S. A. (1998). *The thin book of Appreciative Inquiry.* Bend, OR: Thin Book Publishing Co.

O'Keefe, D. J. (1990). *Persuasion: Theory and research.* Thousand Oaks, CA: Sage Publications.

Petty, R. E., & Cacioppo, J. T. (1986). *Communication and persuasion.* New York, NY: Springer-Verlag.

Schwartz, M. D., Dowell, D., Aperi, J., & Kalet, A. (2007). Improving journal club presentations or, I can present that paper in under 10 minutes. Editorial. *ACP Journal Club, 147*(1), A-8, A-9.

Segal, J., Smith, M., Boose, G., & Jaffe, J. (2013, February 3). Nonverbal communication: Improving your nonverbal skills and reading body language. Retrieved from Helpguide.org.

Sheldon, L., Barrett, R., & Ellington, L. (2006). Difficult communication in nursing. *Journal of Nursing Scholarship, 38*(2), 141–147.

Sherif, C. W., Kelly, M., Rodgers Jr., H. L., Sarup, G., & Tittler, B. I. (1973). Personal involvement, social judgment, and action. *Journal of Personality and Social Psychology, 27*(3), 311–328.

Simons, H. W. (1976). *Persuasion: Understanding, practice, and analysis.* Boston, MA: Addison-Wesley Pub. Co.

Srivastva, S., & Cooperrider, D. (1990). *Appreciative management and leadership: The power of positive thought and action in organizations.* San Francisco, CA: Jossey-Bass.

Wertheim, E. (1988). *Bodily communication.* New York, NY: Metwen.

Additional Reading

Duarte, N. (2008). *Slide:ology.* Sebastopol, CA: O'Reilly.

Fraser, R. (2012). *The nurse's social media advantage : How making connections and sharing ideas can enhance your nursing practice.* Indianapolis, IN: Sigma Theta Tau International.

Pink, D. (2006). *A whole new mind.* New York, NY: Riverhead Trade.

Reynolds, G. (2008). *Presentations.* Indianapolis, IN: New Riders Press.

Warner, C. (1992). *Treasury of women's quotations.* Englewood Cliffs, NJ: Prentice Hall.

"OUR LIVES BEGIN TO END THE DAY
WE BECOME SILENT ABOUT THINGS
THAT MATTER."

–MARTIN LUTHER KING, JR.

Chapter 9

Advocating for the Nursing Profession

–Susan Wysocki

AFTER READING THIS CHAPTER, YOU WILL BE ABLE TO:

- Identify opportunities for advancing the nursing profession
- Consider "out of nursing" opportunities that can raise the profile of the profession
- Make advocacy efforts more impactful

Most new nursing graduates are focused on mastering their clinical skills. However, as you hone your clinical skills, take the opportunity to make note of the issues that affect patients' lives as well as those that affect the profession.

People who excel at advocacy have what could be called a "fire in the belly" about certain issues or frustrations. Passion and enthusiasm are rarely learned by reading, taking classes, or completing capstone projects. The passionate nursing advocate has built his or her enthusiasm on other life experiences, either from nursing or outside of nursing, that move them to take action. Many people choose an area of practice that has personal meaning for them—something for which they have already been kindling the "fire."

The knowledge you gain from experience makes you a credible advocate for change. When an advocate speaks from experience, whether recommending changes for the profession or for patients, others are more likely to listen. Further, in many cases, the advocate's audience may have no inside knowledge or experience of the particular issue. The nurse's influence comes from being able to tell the story that goes beyond the facts.

Patient-centered arguments are much more powerful than other arguments for why something is needed for the profession. To begin with, nurses are better at, and oriented toward, keeping the patient front and center.

IN REAL LIFE:

Two NPs, Lucy and Jane, meet with their state legislators to advocate for prescribing scheduled drugs. Due to a high rate of prescription drug abuse, the state legislature is proposing that NPs should not prescribe these drugs in an attempt to limit the number of prescribers. The state medical association supports the measure, stating that NPs do not have the knowledge base needed to prescribe scheduled drugs. What the legislators do not understand is that NPs staff many of the services in the state's rural areas and inner cities.

NPs Lucy and Jane describe a compelling scenario in which a patient would suffer because of this proposed legislation. The new law would require the NP to contact an MD who would prescribe or dispense scheduled drugs whenever a patient presents with pain. In some cases, the drug will only be filled if the prescription is written— not called in or faxed. This does not mean the pain medication won't be prescribed, but it does mean a delay for the patient to get appropriate pain control. In fact, delaying treatment may escalate the pain and the need for more medication.

Be Prepared

In the vignette above, NP Lucy is questioned about NP qualifications for prescribing narcotics. Lucy provides the answer: "NPs have master's or doctoral level education." Not a very compelling response to reassure the legislator about patient safety. By contrast, NP Jane is prepared. When asked the same question, she provides the pharmacology curricula from the NP schools in the state, pointing out the courses in which controlled substances are discussed. She also reminds the legislator that she is required by the state to attend continuing education pharmacology courses that include content in controlled substances to maintain her license. She brings her personal portfolio of her continuing education and a sample of some of her other colleagues' pharmacology CE portfolios. Whose argument is more impactful?

Illustrate the Problem With More Than Facts

A speaker talking on the topic of gun violence started his speech by placing a sneaker on the podium and then proceeded to give his talk. This created great curiosity for the audience. He gave facts about violence—how often it happened, who was affected, different kinds of violence, and how to recognize it. At the end of his talk, he held up the sneaker and told the audience that it belonged to a boy killed at Columbine. Imagine the impact he made with that disclosure. The sneaker brought the statistics alive and gave them meaning the audience could relate to.

Think creatively. What can you do to give meaning to the points you want to make? It should be something more than facts or statistics. Facts and data reach the logical part of the brain. What can you do to reach the part of the brain that reacts and evokes the audience's feelings? For example, we can know many things about cancer. We can know that more than 1,500 people will die from cancer every day. However, we have a deeper understanding if we have experienced cancer ourselves or have known a family member or close friend who dealt with cancer. Can you think of anyone, including yourself, who has not felt the effects of some health issue? You name it—heart condition, cancer, mental illness, substance abuse, domestic violence, a sick parent or grandparent, a sick child, the list goes on. How can you relate what you are advocating for to your audience's experiences? They don't have to be exactly the same. Know your audience, because the strongest champions for your issue are those who have, or have had, some stake in it. Sometimes all it takes is pointing out to them how much of a stake they have in your issue.

What is in it for them, even when it comes to things such as patient to nurse ratios or nurse incentives (salary and benefits, etc.)? Does anyone want a loved one or themselves to be at risk because not enough nurses are available to care for them? Do people want their nurse to be exhausted by multiple double shifts or an overwhelming number of people to care for, compromising their performance and attention?

IN REAL LIFE:

The ratio of school nurses to students and schools is inadequate for the kind of complex health problems that students have, such as asthma, obesity, diabetes, hypertension, and other health and social problems. A nurse wants help from the state to change this situation. For her meeting with state legislators, she brings along one of the teachers from the schools, and, better yet, she brings along a parent of a child directly affected by this shortage. The child has a condition that led to a health crisis when the school nurse was at another school.

In providing these perspectives, the nurse created opportunities for the legislators to relate to the issue. They may relate with the overworked nurse or the teacher who was unequipped to deal with the health crisis or, especially if they or someone they know has children or grandchildren who could also be affected, they may sympathize with the parent whose child was vulnerable because of the ratio of school nurses to students.

Make No Assumptions About Your Audience

Although the nursing profession is gaining more and more attention, many people, even those with considerable interest in health care, are not fully aware of what nurses are capable of doing or the specialties nurses practice. The alphabet soup of nursing credentials is more than a little confusing. A physicians is an MD—easy. A nurses can be an RN, APRN, CCRN, CNL, CRNA, CNM, FNPs, NCSN. My point is this: Most people have only their own experience of what a nurse does. They do not have the experience of all the roles that nurses play. Beginning the conversation with "Nurses have many roles today; what experiences have you had with nurses?" gives you a starting point to add to what they know.

Consider inviting local, state, and national legislators and other policymakers to your place of work, if appropriate, or to a meeting with your professional colleagues (chapters of nursing organizations, etc.). At the very least, the individual you invite will do some premeeting research about the nursing profession, the practice, the hospital, or other health care settings. Providing an opportunity to observe what a nurse does or exposure to the multiple roles nurses have can be very helpful in educating about the depth and breadth of the nursing profession.

Be a Resource

Any relationship is give and take. Often this point is forgotten when talking to someone such as a legislator or other stakeholder you are trying to influence. Health care today is very complex. In addition to having insights about how the health care system works (or doesn't work), you have unique insights into whatever community you share with the stakeholder (constituents, customers, etc.). Your insights as well as your connections can be invaluable resources to a stakeholder. Don't neglect the resources you have to offer as an exchange for help with your issue. Business cards are essential. A list of other resources—such as local nursing chapter or state and national organizations—offers help up front.

When interfacing in the policy arena, understand that at higher levels of office you may be meeting or communicating with a staff person. This can be an advantage, particularly if the staff person's area of focus is health versus, for example, a member of Congress whose focus is divided into multiple areas. Establishing a relationship as a resource for staff can be even more important. Staff members want to be a resource for their boss.

IN REAL LIFE:

Nurse midwife Rose is qualified to provide pregnancy care to low-income rural women near the border of two states. State A has a supervision requirement. State B does not. Rose, who lives in state A, has spent a year looking for a supervising physician. Among other challenges, very few physicians are close to where she lives, and there are no OB/GYNs. Rose is considering moving to state B.

Because of the limitation of requiring supervision, state A has created an access problem that is likely costing the state millions in poor pregnancy outcomes as well as costs associated with supporting low-income families. State A has a very strong medical society and a conservative legislature and is bogged down in old ways, recalcitrant to change. However, the Affordable Care Act will likely drive changes in the future. Does Rose stay and wait it out to work with a population she has "fire in her belly" to help or move to state B, where she can practice the way she wants to? What could Rose bring to the table to change this situation?

Disruptive Innovations

In 2002, *Harvard Business Review* published an article entitled, "Will Disruptive Innovations Cure Health Care?" by Christensen, Bohmer, and Kenagy, who write that health care institutions have "overshot" the level of care most patients need by having physicians, particularly specialized physicians, providing routine, episodic, and chronic care.

In this must-read article, Christensen, Bohmer, and Kenagy describe how the health care system wastes resources by using physicians who are educated to care for very complex problems and interventions, such as surgery, for the care of patients whose needs do not match the physician's skill set but do match the skill set of nurse practitioners (and, I would suggest, all nurses).

Christensen, Bohmer, and Kenagy define a disruptive innovation as a new idea that replaces (disrupts) an outdated model because it is more efficient, user friendly, accessible, and cost effective (2002). As an example of a disruptive innovation in business, he cites the move from mainframe computers to personal computers. Only a few people needed or could even access a mainframe computer. In contrast, personal computers (PCs) are accessible, user friendly, and are used by the masses. Nurses, like personal computers, offer many of those same qualities of accessibility, user friendliness, etc.

IN REAL LIFE: SUSAN WYSOCKI

Early in my career as a nurse practitioner, I worked in a publicly funded family planning clinic. My ability to care for the women who came to the clinic depended on funds allocated at the state and national level. At some point, I realized that many of the women I cared for had no voice for expressing how important the services were for them. They were statistics to the people who were making decisions about the most intimate aspects of their lives.

So, I became involved with an organization that focused on family planning policy. I was one of the only NPs among mostly administrators. I saw that even though these administrators worked in clinics, they were not behind the closed door of the exam room. They did not have the same insights I did about our clients. I became more convinced that what I could bring to the table was unique.

Working with state legislators, I learned that even a few letters from constituents, who made this important issue relatable, made an impression with them. I learned that they needed helpful insight for making decisions and for writing legislation.

As time went on, I moved to Washington to be closer to the national action. I worked with nurses from various roles and specialties who had similar goals in strategizing to make the changes we wanted for the profession. We often met at my or someone else's home and called ourselves the "Kitchen Cabinet." I continued to broaden my horizons and sought to know people who could influence policies directly or indirectly. One connection led to another.

continues

continued

I was the first staff person for an NP organization that had few resources or members. My passion for women's health and the profession drove me to do whatever was necessary. At times, I traded my consulting services for office space and whatever else it took. No task was too small. I networked with other nurses and whomever I found that could have a possible influence on my profession. But the hard work pays off when you receive a phone call like I did from a pharmaceutical executive who was responding to letters sent by other NPs who were displeased, to say the least, that all of the company's TV ads said, "Only your doctor can..." When they asked me how they should respond, I told them to change the ads to "Ask your health professional." The company did change the ads. I want to thank those who wrote the letters that made that possible.

I want to give my deep appreciation for those teachers, mentors, and health care professionals who paved the way for me by bringing the nursing profession, as well as the role of women in society, to a place where we could be so bold as to create the nurse practitioner role and the role of the women's health nurse practitioner in particular. It doesn't stop at those who were most visible or even visible at all. There is a whole cast and crew who made that possible.

Working With Organizations: Think Outside the Box

Joining and working to enhance the profession through nursing organizations are important. However, networking with other organizations unrelated to nursing can often have a more profound effect on change. A nurse has endless possibilities to work with organizations outside the field of nursing to effect positive change. These include civic groups, school boards, town councils, patient advocacy groups, local and national organizations focused on health issues that are not exclusive to nurses, and, dare I say it, industries such as pharmaceutical companies. You name it. Branching out beyond nursing can help the community, expand the nurse's horizons, and facilitate strategic alliances and connections, resulting in building influence and a power base.

Participating in Nursing Organizations

EVERY nurse should, at the very least, become a member of the nursing organizations that represent their interests. All politics is local. Since states govern what a licensed profession can do in that state, at the barest minimum, joining a local or state nursing group is essential for making the efforts of those state organizations or chapters more potent.

Join a national organization to support the profession, network with other nurses, and learn of opportunities where workshops on developing advocacy skills are being offered. Both state and national nursing organizations have opportunities for participating in lobbying efforts. They may also offer professional development opportunities as well as continuing education. Specialty organizations are important for dealing with issues specific to your role and patient population and for keeping current with the specialty.

After joining, what's next? A number of ways to become involved exist beyond just being a member. Start with participating in the organization's meetings to gain a better understanding about the organization's goals and objectives and to network with others. All organizations have committees or projects looking for volunteers. Sign up. Opportunities range from writing about activities affecting nursing in local areas to being on a conference planning or policy committee, just to name a few. Find a good mentor in the organization to help you learn the ins and outs. And mentor others.

If you are not a member of an organization, that organization is not obligated "in the sake of the profession" to provide you services, advice, or support paid for by someone else in your profession, i.e., the members. It is your responsibility as a professional to carry some of the load, even if you are just paying dues.

Don't expect to be at the top of an organization when you first start out. Experience and knowledge are needed more than personal ambition. At some point, you might want to run for a board or an office at the state or national level. Be clear about why you want to be involved at this level of participation. If your interest is to advance your career and not the goals of the organization, perhaps running for a board position or office is not in the organization's best interests. There are other venues to advance a career. Expect to contribute in "sweat equity" and by making a personally significant financial contribution to the organization. Give what you can, even if it is modest. Don't think that any job to support an organization is too small. At this level in an organization, if you cannot contribute in a real way, you may not be an asset to the organization. Board service should support the organization and help direct policy decisions. Organizations with staff do not need micromanaging of daily operations. Do not be on a board because you want a check mark on your CV.

Final Thoughts

The nursing profession currently has the opportunity to make leaps and bounds with all the attention being given to health care reform and improved access to care for patients. Tread thoughtfully and carefully. Participate in that growth through your own efforts and example, whatever they may be.

References

Christensen, C., Bohmer, R., & Kenagy, J. (2002). Will disruptive innovations cure health care? *Harvard Business Review.* Retrieved from www.hbr.org

"WE CANNOT THINK OF BEING
ACCEPTABLE TO OTHERS UNTIL WE
HAVE FIRST PROVEN ACCEPTABLE TO
OURSELVES."

–MALCOLM X

Chapter 10
How to Act Powerfully

*Melanie Dreher, Cynthia Barginere,
Susan A. Clark, and Benson Wright*

**AFTER READING THIS CHAPTER, YOU WILL BE
ABLE TO:**

- Identify specific ways to act more powerfully in your nursing role
- Take steps to become more politically active
- Understand the importance of empowerment at the bedside

From the bedside to the boardroom, nurses must act powerfully on behalf of patients and the profession regardless of practice setting. In today's challenging health care environment, acting powerfully is more of an imperative than just something to consider from time to time. Acting powerfully is about demonstrating expertise and communicating with pride and confidence while exerting influence in ways that will capture the attention of others. The following experts offer their perspectives on what it means to act powerfully.

Act Like You Mean It

Nursing needs to develop some professional swagger. Just like the line in the Carly Simon song "You're So Vain," nurses should learn how to "walk into the party like you were walking onto a yacht"—proud, in control, and with authority.

Statements such as "I am just a nurse" or "They will never let us do that" bring to light the professional insecurities many nurses face. People who are powerful never say, "I am just a...." That phrase indicates you do not value your own opinion and expertise and will defer decisions and power to others. It means you are not operating to the fullest scope of your professional licensure and are not confident in your contributions as a health care provider.

Whenever I hear the phrase "I am just a nurse," I interrupt the speaker and remind her that she is "THE nurse" and therefore an authority figure on the profession of nursing. Nurses, all of us, are experts in relationships and compassion. We are technical experts, critical thinkers, and evidence-based practitioners. Above all, we are patient advocates and leaders. Nurses are autonomous providers able to make clinical decisions and provide clinical opinions based on the body of nursing knowledge.

Another cringe-worthy statement I frequently hear in nursing committee meetings is, "They will never let us do that." This statement communicates that nurses must seek validation from others to push for improvements in quality, safety, work environment, and patient care. It also demonstrates a collective mentality of oppression.

When faced with a matter important to their profession or work environment, would a room of lawyers, physicians, or executives say, "They will never let us do that"? No. They would develop a plan, advocate, and demand the changes they feel are warranted. They would act with intention and authority. They would speak up and gather support for their cause. Nursing should pay attention.

In committees or groups when someone says, "They will never let us do that," I challenge the speaker with a series of questions. Who is the elusive "they" that will prevent you from taking action? Is the decision that you seek to make within the scope of your practice and within your control? If the decision requires support from others, what grounds do we have to advocate for what is right? In my experience, often there is no "they," and it is nursing that assumes a position of powerlessness in decision making

–Benson Wright

Introduce Yourself With Pride

For 13 of the last 14 years, nurses have been voted the most trusted profession, according to the annual Gallup Honesty and Ethics of Professions poll (Gallup, 2012). We nurses take great pride in being the honest brokers of the health care system; most of us are salaried and do not derive personal gain from ordering expensive tests or procedures. Patients and their families, in the midst of having their lives torn apart by disease, death, social dislocations, or developmental crises, look to nurses to bring order to their chaos.

At the same time, the Institute of Medicine's influential 2011 report, *The Future of Nursing: Leading Change, Advancing Health,* reported that the American public views nursing as the least influential in shaping the health care system, despite being the largest health profession with the greatest patient contact (Institute of Medicine, 2011). The bottom line is that Americans view nursing as the most trusted but the least powerful profession.

The evidence of the profession's lack of power is compelling: Nurses make up only 5% of the governing boards of health care institutions and a disproportionately tiny percentage of C-suites. In addition, state by state, the capacity of advanced practice registered nurses (APRNs or APNs) is diminished by the power of other professions.

The tension inherent in being regarded as most trusted but least influential reflects our professional confusion and discomfort with the notion of power. Nurses want recognition for the work they do. Yet, as a profession, they demure from assuming the personal leadership attributes and behaviors that, in our culture, are commonly associated with influence and authority. They shy away from talking about their accomplishments instead of stepping into the limelight and speaking up with credibility and confidence.

Becoming powerful begins with how we refer to and introduce ourselves to others. Often, we unwittingly hide our own power from the very people from whom our authority derives and who need our influence in health care the most—our patients.

For example, I recently witnessed the reluctance of a doctor of nursing practice-prepared nurse to introduce herself as "doctor." Physicians never relinquish their identification as doctor. Even the youngest medical school graduates introduce themselves by their last names preceded by "doctor," while expert nurses, practicing for 20 years, are "Enid," "Michelle," "Louise," etc. In our society, last names signify adults and employers; first names signify children and workers, thus codifying the generally endorsed power gradient between physicians and nurses.

For the sake of our patients, we can begin the journey of acting powerfully by talking about ourselves with authority, as the following examples show:

Change "Hi, my name is Marie. I'm one of the nurses" to "Hi, Mr. Covington, my name is Ms. Callahan, and I am your nurse today. I have assisted several patients through this procedure before. Please feel free to ask me any questions. Some of my patients feel more comfortable calling me by my first name, Marie, and you are welcome to do so."

"Hi, I'm Julie, the nurse practitioner," to "Hello Mrs. Carlson, I'm Dr. Ortiz. I'm your nurse practitioner, and we're going to begin with you telling me why you're here today. Please let me know what you would like to be called, and you are welcome to call me by my first name, Julie. Or you can call me Dr. Ortiz, whichever you prefer."

"Hi, Dr. Miller. This is Bob on 7 West. Your patient, Mr. Foreman, is having difficulty sleeping and I need an order for medication to help him," to "Hello, Dr. Miller, this is Bob Gaston. I'm the nurse who is managing the care of your patient, Mr. Foreman, and I need your consultation on his inability to sleep. We've reduced any interruptions during the night that aren't absolutely necessary, but I would like to have a medication ready in case he needs it."

Transforming nursing into a profession with more influence will require every nurse to think, act, and believe that he or she is indeed in a position of power. We know that our authority and credibility are derived in our therapeutic interactions with constituents, and we owe it to the individuals, families, and communities for whom we care to act powerfully on their behalf.

–Melanie Dreher

Be Empowered at the Bedside

Nursing has long struggled with the concept of value. What is the best way to demonstrate the value of nursing? Should nursing hours and cost be a single line item on the hospital bill? Will that give patients a better understanding of the value of the care they received? The fact is that patients do recognize the value of the nursing care they receive and the nurses who deliver that care, as the Gallup Poll indicates.

Not only does the public understand the power and importance of nursing care, so does the government. As Medicare and the Affordable Care Act reforms move throughout the health care industry, the importance of the outcomes of care is evident as the Centers for Medicare and Medicaid Services (CMS) continue to roll out value-based purchasing.

Many of the outcome indicators used for value-based purchasing are considered nurse-sensitive indicators. These nurse-sensitive indicators in the acute care setting are outcome measures that are influenced by nursing practice, such as falls, pressure ulcers, patient experience with nursing care, and bacteremia caused by central lines and urinary catheters. Each of these indicators is associated with an incentive or reward payment structure defined by CMS for hospitals and health care providers (Kavanagh, Cimiotti, Abulsalem, & Coty, 2012).

Over time, CMS will increase the number of value-based purchasing indicators and continue to ensure that hospitals and health systems are focused on the quality of the care they deliver, not simply the processes of care.

This provides a unique opportunity for nursing. Not only is the quality and availability of nursing care critical to the perception of the consumer, it is critical to the financial viability of the organization.

But in order to take advantage of this focus on outcomes, nursing leaders must empower staff at the bedside to be accountable for the care they deliver and provide the work environment that facilitates doing the right thing for patient safety.

One example of a value-based purchasing indicator is patient perception of the timeliness of response to call lights. Patients perceive this process measure as an indicator of the quality of the care they receive in the inpatient setting. In order for nursing staff to consistently meet patients' expectations on this process measure, leadership must ensure that the resources needed for success are available to staff and that there is a culture of accountability that ensures that every staff member sees his or her role in providing a timely response to patients' needs.

Leadership must also ensure that nurses feel safe in taking risks at the bedside in fulfilling their role as patient advocates, for example, in ensuring that all health professionals comply with hand hygiene. Compliance with hand hygiene continues to be a challenge for most institutions. It is such a seemingly simple act. The expectation is that you wash your hands or use hand sanitizer before entering the patient's room and upon exit. As leaders we must ask why so many intelligent providers do not follow these guidelines.

And as nurses we must decide to take the lead in ensuring that hand hygiene compliance is improved in our practice areas and be bold enough to insist that all providers caring for our patients take these precautions to keep our patients safe. Being bold and speaking up to partner providers in the health care setting are the nurse's responsibilities to their patients to keep them safe. The nurse's role of surveillance extends from assessment of clinical condition to assessment of environmental factors that will influence clinical condition.

A key outcome measure for which the influence of nursing care is not disputed is pressure ulcers. The diligence of the nurse and the meticulousness of the care delivered can significantly impact the outcomes for compromised patients.

Yet in order for nurses to meet the challenges of these complex patients, they must have adequate education and training and be able to delegate tasks such as baths, turning, and cleaning of incontinence and assess the degree to which nonlicensed personnel complete these important tasks. This requires the ability to develop relationships and strengthen leadership skills on the part of the bedside nurse.

As nursing leaders, we have a responsibility to provide the resources, skills, and competencies nurses need in order to keep patients safe. It is also the responsibility of leaders to create an accountable work environment that supports doing the right thing for patients every time.

–Cynthia Barginere

Gain Power Through Advocacy, Political Activism, and Politics

Statehouses are breeding grounds for issues important to nurses and their patients, such as patient and workplace safety, staffing requirements, and reimbursement. Yet, when it comes to the political arena, nurses are either silent or judged to be radical for speaking up against powerful medical societies, hospitals, and other stakeholders. It is as if most nurses do not believe that they are credible resources in determining what laws are passed, when in reality, nurses know the most.

I often end my talks on political activism to nursing groups with the phrase, "If you're not at the table, you're on the menu." If you as nurses don't speak up, then hospitals, physicians, and other groups will advance their own agendas.

It is not enough to have assertive spokespersons, such as lobbyists, advocating for sound nursing policy; it takes rank and file nurses to "tell it like it is," explain what they do on a daily basis and what it is like to be a nurse in the health care environment.

As a longtime lobbyist in Illinois for the nursing profession, I can say with certainty that legislators have little idea about nursing issues. And yet, since the mid-1990s, it is the nursing profession leading the way for positive health policy changes, often over the opposition of hospitals, physicians, and other health care groups.

All nurses need to know who their state and federal legislators are and how to reach them. A simple Google search can yield this information. Nurses must then make the effort to reach out to these legislators and talk to them about nursing and ask for their support through personalized letters, phone calls, or visits to their local legislative offices.

Illinois has 167,000 registered nurses (8,000 of whom are APNs). If every one of those licensed nurses met with his or her own legislators, kept in touch with them, and offered to be an expert the legislator could turn to, there would be a sea change in how politicians perceive nursing power.

Political action committees (PACs) offer individuals an opportunity to give small amounts of money specifically for nursing. If, for instance, in Illinois, each nurse gave $10 every year, more than a million dollars would be generated for the nursing PAC annually. That is power in politics. Individually it does not require a large output of money, but vast numbers of nurses can reap huge amounts of political influence.

Nurses and student nurses may say they know little about political activism, otherwise called grassroots lobbying. Yet, grassroots lobbying is done in all aspects of life, whether it is convincing a friend to go to a movie instead of a sporting event, trying to change the due date of a paper in college, getting a patient to turn over and relax for an injection, or trying to convince a legislator to vote the way nursing wants him or her to vote.

Lobbying consists of relationships, linked to negotiation, linked to persuasion. It is part of every nurse's daily activity, whether you realize it or not. The challenge is to take your expertise into the political arena by discussing health care issues with policy decision makers. Then nursing will not just be the most trusted profession but also the most influential.

–Susan A. Clark

References

Gallup. (2012). Honesty/ethics in professions. Retrieved from http://www.gallup.com/poll/1654/honesty-ethics-professions.aspx

Institute of Medicine. (2011). *The future of nursing: Leading change, advancing health.* Washington, D.C.: The National Academies Press.

Kavanagh, K. T., Cimiotti, J. P., Abusalem, S., & Coty, M. (2012). Moving healthcare quality forward with nursing-sensitive value-based purchasing. *Journal of Nursing Scholarship, 44*(4), 385–395.

"THEY MAY FORGET YOUR NAME, BUT THEY WILL NEVER FORGET HOW YOU MADE THEM FEEL."

–MAYA ANGELOU

Chapter 11

Two of Nursing's Finest: Their Personal Journeys

–Linda Burnes Bolton

AFTER READING THIS CHAPTER, YOU WILL BE ABLE TO:

- Identify how to begin a leadership journey
- Pinpoint the most important strategies for professional advancement
- Create a virtual learning community to shape your career

Expressing Your Best as a Leader: Initial Steps on the Journey

Leadership is a practiced art that involves translation of knowledge from specific fields of study and experiences gained over a lifetime. I do not believe that individuals are born leaders. Leading and leadership are competencies acquired, shaped, and influenced by your lifelong journey and the encouragement of others.

As an example, your ability to express your best may come from experiences gained during your childhood and entrance into adulthood. You learned how to address situations and expectations from others' life experiences. Your response to changes in your lifetime and the behaviors you adopted to successfully ride the cycles of change influence your ability to express your best as a leader.

Several decades have passed since I began my leadership journey, and those early experiences continue to shape my personal and professional life today. My first leadership situation was handed to me by my mother when I was 10 years old. At the time, I was the oldest of six children and was responsible for preparing my five siblings, all under the age of 9, for school each day. My parents worked two jobs and relied on me to assure that the "gangbusters," as I fondly called them, were bathed, fed, clothed, and ready for the school bus before 7 a.m.

I developed a plan that assigned each younger child to an older child. The older child would be responsible for assisting with bathing and dressing the younger child before either child could have breakfast. The same system worked after school. The older children could not watch TV or have a snack until they had completed their homework and assisted the kindergartners. I learned early in life the value of teamwork and organization in getting things done. Engaging and leading others are critical to expressing your best as a leader. My experiences at home enabled me to adopt the art of individual and team engagement as core leadership competencies. Later in life, I have applied my learned behavior of engaging individuals to assist others in many situations.

Learning to Lead in the Community

I loved to read and to apply knowledge as a kid. After my parents were divorced, we relocated to Phoenix, Arizona, and lived in a housing project 4 years after my initial leadership experience. Our family had grown, and we sought opportunities to assist other families. Many of the neighborhood kids had similar family situations and often missed school, eventually dropping out. I recognized that something needed to be done in our neighborhood, so I organized an after-school fun learning program to engage students in school with those who had dropped out.

It was a combination of math, reading, and games held at the local YMCA. I used my, by then, eight sisters and brothers to recruit kids from the neighborhood. We paired the children and created projects to engage them in helping each other. The Y provided some materials, and eventually we used the same method I used at age 10, pairing individuals with a peer. I loved teaching math and English and working with peers to advance our community.

The YMCA staff introduced me to a program called Upward Bound, which I joined as a volunteer teacher. I learned the value of modeling the change you want others to adopt. Soon we had multiple junior high and high school students serving as student mentors and leaders. Together, we learned that expressing your best as a leader requires you to be purposeful and intentional. We knew that acquiring knowledge and skills was critical to mitigating the risks associated with poverty and broken homes. We became driven to ensure that our neighborhood and community would be successful. Our sense of purpose enabled each of us to express our best.

GOOD TO KNOW:

My experiences as an adolescent and young adult helped shape my leadership journey and made me realize the importance of early identification of your life's purpose. Once you know the driving purpose in life, you can begin to acquire additional skills, knowledge, and experiences to be your best.

My young leadership experiences caused me to conduct a self-assessment regarding my career choice. I knew that my ability to connect with others could be applied in multiple fields. Nursing had always attracted me, but I had other skills that my school counselors thought would benefit me and society more.

To express your personal best requires a crucial conversation with others about what is known and what is left to be done to become the best in your chosen field. The conversation begins with a series of questions regarding the identification of your driving purpose. I call it identifying your "what":

- What is important to you in life?

- What do you wish to accomplish?

- What are you willing to do to accomplish your life's purpose?

- What are you willing to give up so that your talent and energy remain connected to your primary life's purpose?

- What knowledge must you acquire?

- Which leadership experiences should you pursue?

- Who can assist you?

- How do you create a purposeful network of individuals to work with?

To have knowledge of self requires obtaining feedback from others, including peers, colleagues, family, friends, supervisors, competitors, and mentors. The goal is to conduct a 360-degree analysis of self. Over time, seek honest input from others and use the information to create a journey to self-mastery. The journey to expressing your personal best is a long one with multiple side roads. As you learn about self, it becomes evident which additional knowledge and experiences are required to maintain your leadership acumen.

Being the best is not measured by the number of accolades, positions that you hold, or amount of wealth you accumulate. When you have reached a point on your leadership journey where you can be of assistance and influence a larger sphere of individuals, organizations, and society, then you are on the path to being the best. Your intentions and purposeful work to benefit individuals, populations, and society as a whole are what allows you to do your very best.

Learning to Lead in Your Profession: Strategies for Professional Advancement

As you continue your self-assessment, the next step on your leadership journey is to seek opportunities to lead. Sometimes, a volunteer position is presented and you may ask, "Should I do this?" The alternative question is, "Why not?" Volunteer leadership is one of the best strategies for the practice of learning to lead and for advancement within your profession.

The engagement with others unrelated to your daily work to pursue shared purpose can be very satisfying. Volunteering to chair a committee or task force provides you with the opportunity to practice leading and to receive feedback on your skills.

One of my first leadership opportunities arose when I was a student nurse. I was placed in a pioneer role as the only African American student nurse at Arizona State University in the late '60s.

It was a chaotic time, and I experienced many situations where I was "the only one." It was very important for me, and those who would follow in my footsteps, that I exhibited leadership behaviors beyond my learned experience at the time. I sought out opportunities to lead diverse groups of individuals, to help the impoverished members of our society without access to a usual source of health care, and to assist my colleagues in learning about other ethnic groups. As a community of students and consumers of health care services, we formed a bond that enabled us to achieve our goals. The value of engaging consumers of health care services was brought home to me during my student years. I built on the foundational leadership strategy I had adopted early in life, engaging those who would benefit from my efforts.

Seeking to lead within professional nursing societies was a critical strategy adopted throughout my career. I have served in a variety of leadership roles over my professional lifetime. Here is a sampling of my own volunteer leadership experiences:

Volunteer Leadership Experiences

- International Society on Hypertension in Blacks (ISHIB)
- Upward Bound Volunteer Youth Group Leader, Pilgrim Rest Church
- American Heart Association Advisory Board, Beverly Hills Chapter

- Human Relations Commission, City of Los Angeles
- Coalition for the Homeless
- American Heart Association, Professional Volunteer
- Joint Commission on Accreditation of Healthcare Organizations, National Advisory Council
- National Quality Forum, Nursing Standards Committee
- Commission on Graduates of Foreign Nursing Schools (CGFNS) Committee
- California Hospital Assessment Reporting Taskforce, Board of Directors
- United Way Silver Award Community Award Leader

Progressive leadership positions in organizations are essential to preparing yourself to do your very best as a leader.

Purposeful volunteer leadership strengthens your abilities and prepares you to lead in other situations. The skills I acquired from leading within the Western Institute Consortium for Higher Education in Nursing helped me to guide efforts to increase diversity within nursing. Building on that leadership experience prepared me to lead the Minority Health Professional Council within the University of California Area-Wide Health Education Consortium. My years of volunteer work to increase diversity within health professions and to launch programs to close the gaps in access to health care services and in health outcomes were provided at the state and national level. My work to give my best to organizations that were willing to lead change that would benefit society led to my appointment on several national committees. The recognition I received from consumers, local and national entities, professional societies, and foundations was for being present, providing direction, and showing willingness to take on serious, complex issues. It required me to be competent and to stay on the journey to becoming a master at engaging others, removing barriers, and providing enablers to accomplish goals.

REMEMBER THIS:

If you agree with my premise that leadership is a practiced art, then you must position yourself to lead within your profession.

I have served on multiple national campaigns, editorial boards, and conferences sponsored by professional organizations, including:

- Sigma Theta Tau International
- Western Institute of Nursing
- American Organization of Nurse Executives
- American Nurses Association
- American Academy of Nursing
- California Healthcare Foundation
- California Endowment Foundation
- Joint Commission on Accreditation of Healthcare Organizations National Advisory Committee
- National League for Nursing
- Black Congress on Health, Law and Economics
- National Black Nurses Association
- National Association of Hispanic Nurses
- National Coalition of Ethnic Minority Nurse Associations

I have also served on multiple schools of nursing advisory boards, the Health Resources and Services Administration's National Advisory Committee on Nursing Education and Practice, and several Institute of Medicine committees. At the end of this chapter, I've included additional lists of my leadership experiences across nursing, the public sector, and foundations.

My lifelong pursuit to close the gap in health disparities led me to join multiple consortiums. Building on efforts initiated during my role as president of the Council of Black Nurses, Los Angeles, I helped to reduce the incidence of infant mortality. The Great Beginnings for Black Babies consortium enabled steering committee members to express their best while making significant contributions, resulting in the reduction of infant mortality in the county of Los Angeles. Participation in public efforts to eliminate health and social issues enables nurses to lead outside their clinical boundaries. The ability to engage diverse constituencies, create common ground for discussion and recommendation, and lead the implementation of a program that emerges from consensus building are skills honed from expressing your best as a leader.

My Experience With the Department of Veterans Affairs

I was invited to join a team of health professionals to evaluate the Veterans Affairs nursing system. It was a unique opportunity, and I agreed to accept Secretary Filippi's invitation. The commission was into its first 3 months and struggling to establish an approach for the scope of work. The appointed chair resigned, and I was called upon to lead the commission. My first task was to assess the members' willingness to continue the work under my leadership. I began by listening to their ideas. We changed our approach and went out in the field to hear the voices of the working nurse.

Our charge was to ensure that we represented the expressed concerns of the veterans, nurses, nurse leaders, clinical care and support team members, and executive management. I used my knowledge and skill gained from the American Organization of Nurse Executives Center for Nursing Leadership (CNL) to engage the diverse voices. I have continued to use the competencies acquired from the CNL program to express my best in listening to the diverse voices within organizations and professional societies.

Holding progressive volunteer leadership positions improves your leadership prowess and credibility among diverse constituencies. It is important to examine each opportunity to lead with a series of questions:

- Is the organization's purpose aligned with your personal leadership goals?

- Does the position provide you with an opportunity to expand your knowledge and experience? Will your role be one that contributes to or distracts from the organization's work?

- Is the position a purposeful one that will have value to segments of society?

Leading others in a volunteer role is an excellent strategy on the journey to mastery, to becoming the member who would be president, vice president, secretary, and other leadership roles.

Leading in Society: Creating a Virtual Leadership Community

You cannot become a societal leader before you learn to lead yourself and gain experience as a volunteer leader. Once those steps have been mastered, you can proceed on your societal leadership journey. Expressing your best as a societal leader requires that you commit to leading on behalf of the public. Multiple paths may be taken to lead in society, including holding public office, working in settings that qualify as community benefit under federal designation, and establishing business enterprises to benefit the public.

Societal leaders are recognized for their ability to create a shared dream that others will support. Leading in society requires acquiring knowledge about the policies and practices that are barriers to a healthy society and possessing the skills to work with diverse constituencies to remove those societal behaviors. Purposeful leadership experiences include being responsive to colleagues who request your assistance. I receive multiple requests to serve on advisory boards and dissertation committees, to assist local youth groups, to speak, and to host phone conferences. All require my attention and effort. Over the years, my virtual leadership community has grown from experiences and engagements across the nation.

My leadership experiences in society have included serving as a follower and then as a leader. Many opportunities exist to exert one's leadership capabilities in society. The key is to inform others that you are willing to accept the leadership baton. It begins wherever you are in life. For example, you may be in transition between paid employment as a leader, and an opportunity exists to apply your knowledge and skills. Take it. Every step you take on the journey to leadership mastery enables you to express your best as a leader in multiple settings.

Nurse leaders are essential members of the grand society of leaders who are willing to stand up and lead for the expressed purpose of helping to co-create a better place for all to live, work, and play. I am a member of the purposeful leadership communities that exist within the health and social professions. We share the same goal: to be of use to others. We notify other members of leadership and volunteer opportunities to connect and enlarge our community of purposeful leaders.

Expressing your best as a leader includes sharing leadership knowledge and skills, coaching and mentoring others, and modeling the commitment to being of use to the larger society. Being the best is "the why" that encourages and drives us to remain purposeful. Nurse leaders describe their success as being the best purposeful leaders of teams connected to achieving goals that would benefit the larger public

There are many paths to leadership, and to express your best necessitates a willingness to gain knowledge from each path you have taken over a lifetime. Creating a virtual community of leaders from different occupations, genders, ethnicities, nationalities, and perspectives provides you with multiple opportunities to learn and grow. Nurse leaders are first good leaders who have intertwined the knowledge, skill, and commitment gained from the profession of nursing with the knowledge and skills acquired from leading. We are driven by the quest to be the best, not for ourselves, but for others. It is our duty—the essence of nursing—to provide human caring at the individual, population, and societal levels. It is nursing leadership at its very best.

Nursing Leadership

Taking your own path to leadership is an adventure. From leadership organizations to public sector volunteer leadership to nursing foundations, there are many ways to get involved. Search these lists as a starting point for exploring organizations with which you can engage and hone your leadership skills and expertise.

Leadership Organizations

- Council of Black Nurses, Los Angeles: committee chair, secretary, vice president, president

- National Black Nurses Association: multiple committee chair roles, treasurer, vice president, president

- Visiting Nursing & Advisory Council (Duke, Yale, UCLA, UC Davis, Case Western)

- Association of California Nurse Leaders, health committee chair

- American Academy of Nursing: multiple committee chairs, secretary, president

- American Nurses Association, National Advisory Council on Nursing
- American Organization of Nurse Executives: committee chair, board of directors
- National Black Nurses Foundation, board of directors
- YWCA committee chair
- Recruitment & Retention Committee chair:
  - Arizona State University
  - UCLA School of Nursing
  - UCLA School of Public Health
- UCLA School of Nursing dean search committee
- National League for Nursing accreditation committee
- American Academy of Nursing, chair, public relations committee
- ONE California, chair, healthy communities committee
- Yale School of Nursing, external advisory board
- Duke University School of Nursing, advisory board

Public Sector Volunteer Leadership

- Vice Chair of the Committee on the Robert Wood Johnson Foundation Initiative on the Future of Nursing
- Health Brain Trust
- Health Resources and Services Administration Grant Review Committee, Division of Nursing
- Health Resources and Services Administration, Maternal Child Health Division
- Healthy People 2000 Review
- Institute of Medicine committees
- National Advisory Council on Nursing Education
- National Heart, Lung, and Blood Institute: Advisory Council on Cholesterol Education
- Bureau of Health Professions, National Advisory Council on Nursing Education & Practice

- Veterans Administration, Expert Panel on Clinical Guidelines & Pathways
- National Cholesterol Education Program, NHBL
- Institute of Medicine, Expert Panel on Nursing Research in the Military
- Institute of Medicine, Committee on Quality Chasm, Next Step Summit
- Title VIII Funding Methodology Commission, Division of Nursing, Bureau of Health Professions
- Assemblyman Paul Koretz (D), California Nursing Taskforce

Foundations

- California Health Care Foundation, Leadership Advisory Board
- California Institute for Nursing & Healthcare
- Health Care Reform
- Kellogg Foundation
- National Black Nurses Foundation
- Robert Wood Johnson Foundation, trustee
- Case Western Reserve University, trustee

Additional Reading

Baldwin, C. (1998). *Calling the circle: The first and future culture.* New York, NY: Bantam.

Carnegie, M. E. (1995). *The path we tread: Blacks in nursing worldwide, 1854–1994* (3rd ed.). New York, NY: National League for Nursing Press.

Institute of Medicine. (2011) *The future of nursing: Leading change, advancing health.* Washington, DC: The National Academies Press.

Nelson, S., & Rafferty, A. M. (2010). *Notes on Nightingale.* Ithaca, NY: Cornell University Press.

Nightingale, F. (1858). *Notes on nursing.* New York, NY: Kaplan.

Patterson, K., Grenny, J., Maxfield, D., McMillan, R., & Switzler, A. (2008). *Influencer: The power to change anything.* New York, NY: McGraw-Hill.

"MY MISSION IN LIFE IS NOT MERELY
TO SURVIVE, BUT TO THRIVE, AND
TO DO SO WITH SOME PASSION, SOME
COMPASSION, SOME HUMOR, AND
SOME STYLE."

–MAYA ANGELOU

The Dynamics of Leadership: A Personal Perspective

–Barbara Nichols

Leadership, like marriage, is a relationship. It is a topic that intrigues women in general and nurses in particular. At some point many have asked: What is it that makes leaders? How do I get into a leadership position? Once there, how do I sustain the role?

So what have I learned about leadership? Plenty. My objective is to share my experience as the first Black president of the American Nurses Association (ANA) in its 100-year history. My story is both personal and relative. My comments speak to leadership positions in general but especially for women of color. It is my hope that personal analysis of my leadership role will prove to be both informative and instructive.

During the 1970s and 1980s, American women were excelling in sports, entertainment, and medicine. For the first time in history, women reached new heights in the corporate world. In 1978, Hannah H. Gray, a German-American, became the first president of a major research university–Chicago University. In the same year, seemingly out of nowhere, Nancy Lopez, a Mexican-American, became the star of women's professional golf. Like these women, I also faced new challenges and choices in the unfamiliar terrain of leadership.

As I talk about leadership from the perspective of being the first Black president of the ANA, think about the politics of leadership. Think about how leadership relates to class, age, gender, stereotypes, race, conflict, organizational politics, and pressure. Think about the economics of power, the costs of power (psychological and financial), and the opportunities afforded by power. In this context, the ingredients for power must consist of desire, broad thinking, possession of some form of capital (be it money or even an asset such as education), the ability to sacrifice and, on occasion, neurotic behavior. Think about Darwin's theory—the fittest survive.

I conclude that if you are a minority in a leadership position, overcoming stereotypes and collective guilt is the underbelly of success. The challenge for all minorities holding leadership positions is to figure out how to be a success but not a sellout to your ethnicity. In my situation, it was how to maintain my individuality but not abandon my spirit of Black community. How to be Black but integrated, whole, and yet always a part of the collective nursing community.

When I announced that I was going to run for the presidency of ANA, only two states supported me: Oregon and Wisconsin. The Wisconsin nurses seemed to support my ideas, and their devotion to a common cause was fascinating. These nurses were actively involved in my campaign on all levels, from fundraising to lobbying for me across the country. They provided immeasurable psychological, physical, and financial support from beginning to end.

An interesting difference emerged, however, when I asked the Oregon nurses why they supported me, and they expressed that they didn't really know. They simply followed the lead of their executive director. For their sake, we can only hope that I met their expectations as an effective and worthy leader. At the time of the election, I was a member of the ANA board of directors. However, not one board member supported me. The board members stated that I was not old enough, I was not experienced enough, I was not yet ready, and I did not look "presidential."

The bylaws of the association at the time stated that to be eligible to run for office, one must be a member of the association and willing to serve if elected. It contained no reference to age or physical appearance. Thinking back, I have always wondered why women in leadership positions are held to different standards. We are all guilty in a sense that upon first thought, we imagine female leaders to be older, faceless, and rigid. The truth is that all women, regardless of color, are virtually frozen out of influential positions in the corporate, governmental, and academic world if they are slightly quirky, young, attractive, or ethnic and fun-loving.

A point of advice: To be successful in any endeavor, you must learn the art of capitalizing on your individuality but more importantly, learn to be a thinker. Stay several steps ahead of your adversaries and get behind your allies. Learn how to use intuitive elements of survival in order to achieve success. This I believe will serve you longer than any other physical or personality trait.

If you have not had the advantages of the elite, you can still rise to the head of the class. It may take longer because you may not have role models or access to shortcuts. Yet, in my case, no groundswell of folks stepped forward to help me learn the ropes; I learned from my own experience.

I was elected president of ANA in 1978 and reelected in 1980. I served two consecutive 2-year terms and completed my second term in July of 1982.

The presidency of the largest nursing organization in America is a grand and personal odyssey. It offers excitement, status, prestige, and immeasurable opportunity to experience the depth and breadth of nursing. It also offers the opportunity to be part of the formulation of health policy in this nation. I am forever indebted to the nurses of America, who granted me the privilege to represent them.

What have I learned? On a personal level, I learned that others do not necessarily desire that you become successful, often because the personal success of one can suggest the subservience of others. For this reason, I am convinced that success is not handed to anyone on a silver platter. One must learn how to accept rejection while holding on to personal goals.

Learn to be self-motivated. Learn that it is imperative to have knowledge and skills and essential expertise as it relates to issues and trends in your professional field. Learn to appreciate all aspects of the programs you will manage and supervise. Know that the road to success is paved with isolation, social and domestic sacrifices, feelings of vulnerability, exhaustion, dual roles, and many sleepless nights.

I've learned an invaluable concept about power. I've learned that power is not a commodity like money, or something that one can accumulate and store up for use whenever one likes. You must use power while you have it or you will lose it. Experience has taught me that when it is all said and done, companies, organizations, and governments do not really grant titles and powers to women because they are kind and good, or even as a mandate of affirmative action. Women get powerful leadership positions because they are ambitious, competent, intuitive, patient, and persistent! Power is the control, impact, and influence you demonstrate at a moment's notice—unrehearsed, original, and against all odds. I have always been powerful. Being elected president of ANA was just another manifestation of that reality.

Now let me share with you my leadership lessons learned:

1. Know Thyself

Know your values; a personal philosophy allows you to remain grounded.

Understand your personal strengths and limitations; build on your assets.

Understand that failure is not fatal; you can be successful without being perfect.

Learn how to be self motivated; accept rejection, while holding fast to goals.

Monitor your thinking so that you are reflective; do not dismiss the positive or hold onto the negative.

2. Prepare to Achieve Your Goal

Relentlessly obtain the knowledge, skill, essential expertise, and validated competencies that relate to the defined areas of your professional work.

Prepare, prepare prepare; we seldom succeed by winging it.

3. Learn to be Strategic

It is important to understand that both the journey and the destination are important.

Keep your goal in mind when adapting your strategy to circumstances.

Think strategically big; make your efforts worth the investment. Remember, strategic thinking enables you to achieve your vision through goal implementation.

4. Create Partnerships

Creating partnerships through collaboration is the engine that fuels both change and goal achievement.

You accomplish more and have greater impact when you partner with others.

Develop the knowledge and skills to foster partnerships.

Refine and perfect your communication skills.

5. Teamwork

Build effective teams with:

Mutual respect—appreciating the skills and attitudes each teammate brings

"We" thinking—looking for ways to utilize the collective resources of the team for the most successful outcome

Ownership—embracing the goals of the initiative

Flexible leadership—enabling different teammates to emerge as leaders whenever the situation calls for it

6. Legislative Policy and Practices

Become familiar with the political process—this requires persistence and patience.

Establish relationships with legislators at the local, state, and federal levels.

Learn all that you can about local, state, and federal agencies that deal with health care credentialing, licensure, and funding.

Become a resource of knowledge for legislators and staff in both the executive and legislative branches.

7. Dress for Success

Be well groomed. Unfortunately, what you look like and what you wear define you—paraphrasing the psychologists: You only have one time to make a first impression as a leader.

Concluding Thoughts

I've learned an invaluable lesson: Regardless of where you find yourself, eventually you will have to leave the mountaintop. When that time comes, leave with the joy of having had the opportunity to experience the view from the top.

Appendix

Resources for Success

–Debra Werner

This appendix offers tools, techniques, and tips for getting and staying current on your areas of expertise in nursing.

Tools to Keep Current: So Much Information, So Little Time

Hundreds of thousands to millions of scientific papers are published each year (Bjork & Roos, 2009). It can be difficult, overwhelming, and even costly to stay on top of all that information. Which specialty nursing journals should you read? Which medical journals? What about health reports from major news outlets or the government? What about blogs? If you're actively trying to accelerate your career, it's smart to have a strategy to keep abreast of the latest developments in your specialty area, as well as generally, in nursing and medicine.

A number of tools are available to streamline the process of finding information. Many of these tools push or send information directly to a reader, and they are generally referred to as feed reader, RSS reader, or news reader. Once you've set up a feed reader tool, it's much easier to simply develop a habit of checking updates every day.

Technology changes rapidly, and one popular tool may disappear seemingly overnight—as was the case when Google shut down Google Reader in mid 2013—so we suggest you explore several options and pick one that is most comfortable for you. A lot of people have written reviews about feed readers, so don't be shy about doing a web search for "best feed reader," "most popular feed reader," or "easiest feed reader." You'll find a lot of reviews and opinions which you can make use of.

The following sections briefly address technology tools to serve up the information. Again, we do not go into very much detail as the web is full of up-to-the-minute instructions and support to help you through the installation or setup. This appendix is geared toward general knowledge, not specific instructions or recommendations.

RSS

Wouldn't it be nice to be able to read all of your favorite journals and websites from one location, instead of manually bookmarking them and navigating to all the dozens of different locations? RSS, short for Really Simple Syndication, makes this possible. Websites that publish frequent updates usually rely on RSS to push out their updates. So, any time a new issue or article is added to a journal or news website, it is fed to the RSS location. The feed is the stream of new content updates, and is a great way to keep current on health reports from major news sources. We list a number of the popular feed readers below, but remember that this is fast-changing technology so the feed readers and their popularity are subject to change.

- AOL Reader
- Digg
- Feedly
- Feedspot
- Inoreader
- Netvibes
- Newsvibe
- Pulse
- The Old Reader
- Zite

> **NOTE**
>
> *For security purposes, many hospitals or institutions set their computer firewalls to restrict access to feed readers.*

Subscribing to a journal's RSS feed is not the same as subscribing to the journal itself and typically does not provide access to full-text articles for nonsubscribers. Most journals provide RSS feeds to their table of contents for those who have not subscribed to the journal.

> **TIP**
>
> *Keep it manageable. Only subscribe to the feeds that are important and that you will read. Periodically review your feed reader and eliminate those feeds that are no longer useful.*

Alerts

Alerts are email notifications or RSS updates based on parameters that the user sets, such as the results of a saved search or a notification each time a specific article is cited. Alerts are similar to RSS feeds in that they push information directly to you.

The following types of alerts are useful for staying current on the latest information related to a research project or in a specialty:

- Search Alerts: Set up a search in a database and save it. The database will run the search on the schedule you set (hourly, daily, weekly, monthly, etc.) and send new results. Search alerts are particularly useful when doing research where it's important to have the latest information on a very specific subject for the duration of the project. They eliminate the scramble, at the end of the project, of trying to remember the search strategy used months prior and playing catch-up on the new articles that have since been published.

- Author Alerts: Receive notification each time a specific author is cited. Is there an expert in the field whose publications are must-reads? An author alert is the perfect way to stay current on the article output of influential authors.

- Citation Alerts: Receive notification each time a specific article is cited.

- Table of Contents (TOC) Alerts: Receive notification each time a new journal issue is published. An alternative to the RSS feed of new journal issues, discussed earlier, is to receive an email when new issues of favorite journals are published.

Social Media

When Google announced it was canceling Google Reader in July of 2013, its official reason was that usage had declined to the point that Google wanted to redirect elsewhere the resources needed to support Google Reader. In the blogosphere, though, many speculated that it was because more and more people were getting their headline news and information through social media services such as LinkedIn, Facebook, Twitter, YouTube, and Google+. While LinkedIn is most often considered the professional social media site, many organizations and companies send out their news, updates, and alerts through a number of social media channels, foremost among them Facebook and Twitter. This doesn't mean that RSS and alerts are going away; it simply means you can keep up-to-date on your professional world at the same time you're keeping up with family, friends, and other interests. Because of the ever-changing nature of technology, we won't explore how to set up your social media sites to follow professional organizations and resources. They all have robust search engines and "follow" functions. Simply search for what you are looking for and then follow it.

What to Read?

No one has time to read every new study in every specialty and field of interest. Use the strategies outlined in this section to get the most out of the available time to read new research.

Type of Article

While it is important to read original research studies in your specific area of expertise, in many cases you can save time while staying informed by reading review articles and practice guidelines. The authors of review articles and practice guidelines do the labor-intensive work of searching and reviewing the literature and, in some cases, synthesizing it. There are several different types of review articles:

- Systematic review: Offers the highest level of evidence; it seeks to answer a specific clinical question by conducting a comprehensive literature search, including only well-designed studies that meet pre-defined inclusion criteria in its synthesis.

- Meta-analysis: A systematic review that uses statistical methods to combine the results of all the studies.

- Narrative review: Includes a thorough review of the literature, although not as comprehensive as a systematic review. A narrative review is more susceptible to confirmation bias, in which studies that confirm the author's view or hypothesis are preferred and included in the review over those that do not.

Find systematic reviews and meta-analyses:

- Cochrane Database of Systematic Reviews from the Cochrane Library

- PubMed's Clinical Queries limits results to systematic reviews.

- In CINAHL, limit a search to the publication type meta-analysis and/or systematic review.

Find practice guidelines:

- National Guideline Clearinghouse is a free initiative of the Agency for Healthcare Research and Quality (AHRQ), which is a division of the U.S. Department of Health and Human Services.

- JBI Best Practice Information Sheets (subscription required) are produced by the Joanna Briggs Institute, an international not-for-profit research and development organization based at the Faculty of Health Sciences at the University of Adelaide, South Australia.

Deciding Which Journals to Invest Your Time With

In reality, most nurses have very little time to read any articles at all. So, how do you choose which journals to read? Sadly, there's no easy answer. It all depends on your interests and goals (e.g. in-depth, expert knowledge, or basic information). However, there are a few methods for getting started in choosing your journals.

One method, though somewhat controversial, is to use journal rankings, such as Thomson Reuter's Journal Citation Report's Impact Factor, the Eigenfactor, or the SCImago Journal & Country Rank (SJR). These tools are used in an attempt to measure the impact, influence, or prestige of a journal for comparison purposes. They do not provide definitive answers as the methods for calculating the rankings do not work equally well for every journal, and some of the methods are susceptible to manipulation to increase a journal's ranking. Keep in mind that a journal's ranking does not indicate quality at the article level: High-quality articles are published in lower-ranked journals, and mediocre articles are published in highly ranked journals.

The Nursing and Allied Health Resources Section of the Medical Library Association has developed a "Selected List of Nursing Journals" to help evaluate journals. Information about the journal project and a link to the most recent list is at http://nahrs.mlanet.org/home/. The list provides useful information, such as the number of articles each journal publishes and how many of those are systematic reviews, guidelines, or research articles.

Talk to colleagues to learn about journals they read and find useful. And finally, get started researching. The more one searches for articles, the more one understands which journals publish quality articles that are interesting to the reader.

In addition to nursing journals, all nurses should keep up-to-date on information published in general medical journals. Best bets include *The New England Journal of Medicine, The Lancet, The Journal of the American Medical Association (JAMA), PLOS Medicine, BMJ*, and *Annals of Internal Medicine*. All listed journals have RSS and social media feeds, and nearly all provide some free articles. *PLOS Medicine* has open access and is entirely free.

Read Like a Pro

So you've done your homework and now have stacks and stacks (or web bookmark after web bookmark) of journal articles to read, but how do you get through it all? One good technique is to develop a process to tackle the reading in a systematic way and to learn how to discern which articles are worth the time to read.

Efficient Reading

While advice varies on how to efficiently read a research article, there are two constants:

1. Reading an article from start to finish, like a novel, is inefficient.

2. Reading is an active task.

Most advice involves some type of skimming, but the suggestions are sometimes in direct conflict. For instance, read the title versus ignore the title; look at the authors' names versus ignore the authors' names. One system will not work for all, so settle on a process that works for your individual needs. Examples of reading processes written by nurses are found in Raines' (2013) "Reading research articles" and Hudson-Barr's (2004) "Scientific inquiry. How to read a research article." Another worthwhile approach is outlined by Keshav (2007), updated in 2012, at: http://blizzard.cs.uwaterloo.ca/keshav/home/Papers/data/07/paper-reading.pdf.

Reading is active in that the reader should ask questions while reading and take notes. Different types of papers—systematic reviews, qualitative research, randomized controlled trials, etc.—require asking different questions. Examples of questions to ask for each type of paper or study are outlined in Greenhalgh's (2010) book and articles discussed below.

NOTE

For a quick primer on the structure of a research article and what a reader should gain from each section, read Arslanian's Orthopaedic Nursing *article (2000), "Taking the Mystery out of Research: How to Read a Nursing Research Article."*

> **TIP**
>
> *If the terminology commonly found in evidence-based research articles, such as confidence interval (CI), odds ratio (OR), or risk or relative ratio (RR), is a barrier, read Welk's (2007) succinct overview, "How to read, interpret, and understand evidence-based literature statistics."*

Critical Reading

Not all papers are of equal value or importance. Spend time on higher quality articles and skip those of lesser quality. As mentioned previously, a helpful guide to determine which papers are worth your time is *How to Read a Paper: The Basics of Evidence-Based Medicine (4th ed.)*, written by Trisha Greenhalgh and published in 2010 by BMJ Books. It covers levels of evidence, types of studies, methodological quality, statistics for nonstatisticians, and more. Many nurses will find the section titled "Ten Questions to Ask About a Paper Describing a Quality Improvement Initiative" to be quite useful. If you don't have ready access to it, a good alternative—although not as current—is the BMJ series of articles *"How to Read a Paper,"* excerpted from the first edition of the book. The series is available at http://www.bmj.com/about-bmj/resources-readers/publications/how-read-paper.

Keeping Track of What You've Read

Does this scenario sound familiar? You've spent a lot of time finding a good, relevant article, and you've finally found the time to read it, but it's disappeared. It could be in a stack of printed articles, in a folder on a work computer, in a folder on a home computer, on a shared drive at work, in one of several work email accounts, or in one of several personal email accounts. Just as it is important to develop a strategy for finding information, it is similarly important to develop a method for keeping track of it.

Reference Managers

Reference managers, also called citation management software or reference management software, are extremely useful tools for organizing citations and article PDFs, and they are indispensable for research projects. They allow users to add article citations to the reference manager and to organize the citations using folders. Most databases and many journals make it easy to add citations to reference managers by providing an *export* or *export citations* link, which automatically transfers all of the pertinent information (journal title, article title, author, abstract, etc.) to the reference manager. Although PDFs can also be attached to the citation, that is not part of the export process.

While it takes time up front to learn how to use the software, the time-saving organization it provides is worth the investment. The big payoff comes when working on a project. With just a few clicks, you can add your citations to your paper and build the bibliography, formatted in the style of your choice. The time saved in compiling the bibliography and not having to hand-format it yourself is worth the time needed to learn the software. Like RSS readers, reference managers can be web-based or downloadable software, and some, such as Zotero, are freely available. Do a quick web search to find comparisons of the most current reference managers.

Librarians and Libraries: Your Best Friends

Librarians and libraries are tremendous resources for nurses at all levels, whether in early career, going back to school, conducting clinical trials, or somewhere in between. Most librarians are highly service-oriented, and are eager to help others find the information they need. Libraries serve multiple purposes, including to house books, journals, and other materials; to provide a place for quiet study or group collaboration; to provide access to computers and other technology; and to provide support in finding what you are looking for. The physical space occupied by medical libraries varies greatly from one organization to the next. Whatever the size, the mission of every library to provide the resources and services needed by its community is shared.

Available Services

Libraries offer a wide range of services. Unfortunately, those persons who could benefit from these services are often not aware of them. Find out what services are provided at your organization's library, and start using those that will benefit patient care, professional development, and research. If you do not have a library at your organization, refer to the following section on Free and Open Access Resources. Library size and staffing affect what services are offered; here is a list of what libraries and librarians are able to provide:

- Conduct training sessions during in-services, Grand Rounds, or other meetings. Sessions could cover how to do a literature search, how to access ejournals from home, how to find ebooks, how to find the best evidence, etc.

- Perform literature searches and provide citation list (bibliography) and/or articles.

- Locate and summarize articles; send summaries to units or individual nurses.

- Provide consultation to demonstrate how to more effectively use databases or other tools, such as the online catalog or reference management software.

- Offer current awareness services in which the librarian performs the steps outlined in the Keeping Current section on a topic of interest, and routinely sends informational updates.

- Provide consumer health and patient education information that nurses may give to their patients regarding the patient's condition, treatment, etc.

- Answer reference questions through a variety of communication modes: in-person, email, phone, and chat (instant message). Note that in-depth questions are better handled in person during a scheduled appointment.

- Create or compile online tutorials that demonstrate diverse skills, from how to use the CINAHL database to how to use the library printer.

- Create subject guides that you can use to organize necessary resources (databases, journals, etc.) and provide instructions on their use.

- Suggest databases, ebooks, journals, etc., that are useful for specific information needs.

- Assist with research and publishing needs, such as:

  - Using reference management software.

  - Educating authors and users on copyright laws.

  - Suggesting appropriate journals for publication.

  - Providing guidance on complying with the NIH Public Access Policy.

- Request, or show nurses how to request, items owned by other libraries. This service is often called Interlibrary Loan or Document Delivery.

Free and Open Access Resources

If a hospital or organization does not have a library, take advantage of the resources that are freely available. With the growing open access movement, there are many high-quality resources available free online. Open access means that access to and use of an article is free and unrestricted. These resources are useful to those whose hospital or organization does not have a library, as well as to those who do have libraries.

Free resources include:

- The Directory of Open Access Journals at http://www.doaj.org/
- PMC (PubMed Central), a free full-text archive of biomedical journal literature at http://www.ncbi.nlm.nih.gov/pmc/
- Virginia Henderson International Nursing Library's Online Research Repository at http://www.nursinglibrary.org/vhl/

Many librarians create subject guides, which provide quality information about topics such as EBP (evidence-based practice), statistical resources, APA style, and much more.

Here is a tip for finding information on a library's nursing subject guide:

1. In Google, type the topic in the search box.

2. Add the word *library* to the search.

3. Add *site:.edu* to search only within the .edu domain, limiting results to academic institutions.

For example, if you are interested in finding sources for grant funding, try searching "nursing grants library site:.edu." If you want to learn more about appraising evidence, try "nursing appraising evidence library site:.edu."

This technique works well with very broad topics, such as for the evidence-based practice example. Often, however, the more specialized the topic, the fewer results retrieved.

Continuing Education

Earning continuing education (CE) credits is important in maintaining licensure and staying current in your field. Continuing education credits may be earned in a variety of ways. Journals, databases, organizations, and other online tools offer options in a range of CE formats, including text, video, and web- and podcasts. International, national, and local conferences provide excellent opportunities to earn CEs, while programs within one's hospital, such as Grand Rounds, offer a free alternative.

Journals and eJournals

Gone are the days that CE quizzes from print journals needed to be mailed and postmarked prior to an expiration date. Journals still offer CE credits, but many are now available online through ejournals. Here are just some of the nursing ejournals that offer CEs:

- AACN Advanced Critical Care
- American Journal of Critical Care
- American Journal of Nursing
- CIN: Computers, Informatics, Nursing
- Clinical Journal of Oncology Nursing
- Critical Care Nurse
- Journal for Nurse Practitioners
- Journal of Continuing Education in Nursing
- Journal of Nursing Regulation
- Journal of Trauma Nursing
- MCN: The American Journal of Maternal Child Nursing
- MEDSURG Nursing
- Nephrology Nursing Journal
- NurseWeek
- Nursing
- Nursing Economic$
- Nursing Management
- Nursing Spectrum
- Nursing Standard
- Pediatric Nursing

Databases

Some universities and hospitals subscribe to databases and other online resources that facilitate access to CEs, including:

- CINAHL Plus with Full Text
- Mosby's eLearning (part of Mosby's Nursing Suite)
- Nursing Reference Center

Professional Organizations and Associations

There are other online options that do not require institutional subscriptions. Professional associations offer CE credits, and although membership is not always required, members often receive access to some free CE courses.

- The Honor Society of Nursing, Sigma Theta Tau International offers some free CE courses to its memebers. http://www.nursingsociety. org
- ANANurseCE (The American Nurses Association's Center for Continuing Education and Professional Development) offers free CE courses for members http://ananursece.healthstream.com/default. aspx
- The Center for Disease Control and Prevention's Training and Continuing Education Online offers free CE courses https://www2a.cdc. gov/TCEOnline/

Commercial Websites

Commercial websites are another source of CE courses, both free and fee-based. Here are some online options:

- Nurse.com: Some free CE courses http://www.nurse.com
- NursingCenter.com: Fee-based http://www.nursingcenter.com
- CINAHL Education modules: Free CE courses ceu.cinahl.com
- Medscape Nurses Education: Free CE courses http://www.medscape.org/nurses
- Audio-Digest Foundation; Fee-based CE courses http://www.audio-digest.org

Conferences

Most nursing conferences accredited by the American Nurses Credentialing Center confer CE credits for attending presentations and sessions. Set up RSS feeds or alerts with your preferred nursing organizations to keep on top of conference schedules. As an example, The Honor Society of Nursing, Sigma Theta Tau International posts all its upcoming conferences in one location on its website: http://www.nursingsociety.org/STTIEvents/NursingConferences/Pages/NursingConferences.aspx.

Institutional Initiatives

Your institution may provide free and convenient CE offerings. Contact your education or HR departments to explore potential options.

References

Arslanian, C. (2000). Taking the mystery out of research: How to read a nursing research article. *Orthopaedic Nursing, 19*(3), 43-44.

Bjork, B. C., & Roos, A. (2009). Scientific journal publishing: Yearly volume and open access availability. *Information Research, 14*(1), paper 391.

Greenhalgh, T. (2010). *How to read a paper: The basics of evidence-based medicine* (4th ed.). Chichester, West Sussex, UK; Hoboken, NJ: Wiley-Blackwell.

Hudson-Barr, D. (2004). Scientific inquiry. How to read a research article. (Hudson-Barr, D. (Ed.). *Journal for Specialists in Pediatric Nursing, 9*(2), 70-72.

Keshav, S. (2007). How to read a paper. *SIGCOMM Comput. Commun. Rev., 37*(3), 83-84. doi:10.1145/1273445.1273458

Raines, D. (2013). Reading research articles. *Neonatal Network, 32*(1), 52-54. doi:10.1891/0730-0832.32.1.52

Welk, D. (2007). How to read, interpret, and understand evidence-based literature statistics. *Nurse Educator, 32*(1), 16-20.

Index

A

AACH (American Academy on Communication in Healthcare), 6
AACN (American Association of Colleges of Nursing)
    AACN-Wharton Executive Leadership Program, 111-112
    Leadership for Academic Nursing Program, 112
    Student Policy Summit, 112
AACN (American Association of Critical-Care Nurses), 22
AAN (American Academy of Nursing), 47, 49, 111
AANP (American Academy of Nurse Practitioners), 49
accenting, in nonverbal communication, 123
advocacy
    credibility in, 130
    disruptive innovations and, 134-136
    "fire in the belly," 130
    and legislators
        nurses as political activists, 145-146
        nurses as resources for, 132-134, 163
        patient-centered arguments to influence, 130-131
    nurse empowerment and, 145-146
    nursing organizations and, 137-138
    organizations outside nursing and, 136
    preparation for, 131-132
    resources for, 133-134
Affordable Care Act, 134, 143
AHRQ (Agency for Healthcare Research and Quality), 7
Allison, Penne, core value statement, 3-4
ANA (American Nurses Association), 26, 104, 111, 159-161
AONE (American Organization of Nurse Executives), Center for Nursing Leadership, 154
APHA (American Public Health Association), 109
applications, graduate school. See graduate school applications
Appreciative Inquiry, 124-125
Arrien, Angeles (model of sufficiency), 15
Ask Me 3 campaign, 7
awards. See recognition and awards
awareness of self, 16-19

B

bedside nurses
    hand hygiene and, 144
    nurse-sensitive indicators, 143
    pressure ulcers and, 144
Bolton, Linda Burnes
    leadership experiences
        childhood, 148-149
        foundations, 158
        health disparities, 153
        professional organizations, 153, 156-157
        societal leader, 155
        Veterans Affairs nursing system, 154
        virtual leadership community, 155, 156
        volunteer, 151-153, 157-158
    self-assessment of career choices, 150

C

Campbell-Hallam Team Leader Profile (TLP), 11
career foundation, 2-7
CDC (Centers for Disease Control and Prevention), 109, 111
CMS (Centers for Medicare and Medicaid Services), 143
coaching
    coaching considerations, 14-15
    model of sufficiency, 15-19
cognitive dissonance theory (CDT), 120-122
communication
    Appreciative Inquiry, 124-125
    components of clear communication, 115
    importance to nursing, 115
    listening skills, 116-117
    nonverbal communication
        accenting, 123
        complementing, 123
        contradiction, 123
        repetition, 122
        substitution, 123
    persuasion
        central *versus* peripheral messages, 119-120
        cognitive dissonance theory (CDT), 120-122
        definition, 117
        elaboration likelihood model (ELM), 118-119

in group presentations, 125-127
latitudes and, 118
Likert scales, 118
social judgment theory and, 118
self-appraisal and, 6-7
social networking, 123-124
time restraints, 116
Toastmasters, 116
complementing, in nonverbal
communication, 123
Connaughton, Mary J., core value statement,
3
contradiction, in nonverbal communication,
123
core value statements, 3-5
core values, 2-5
credentials, nursing, 133
curriculum vitae (CV). *See also* portfolios,
resumes
definition, 32
versus resume, 32
topics included, 32

D

DiSC Classic, 11

E

educators, nurse, 4, 5, 114
elaboration likelihood model (ELM),
118-119
Emergenetics Profile, 11
empowerment of nurses
advocacy and, 145-146
bedside nurses
hand hygiene and, 144
nurse-sensitive indicators, 143
pressure ulcers and, 144
"I am just a nurse," 140
lack of power in nursing, 141-142
need for, 140
perspectives on, 140-146
politics, 145-146
talking with authority, 142
"They will never let us do that,"
140-141
endorsements. *See* recommendations
EQ Map, 11
essays, for graduate school applications
effective essay example, 87-88
ineffective essay example, 88-89
Organized, 86
Professional, 87
Singularity, 86
STOP acronym, 85
Tailored, 86

F

feedback
after interview, 108
on resumes, 105
self-assessment and, 51, 150
fellowships. *See also* internships, residencies
applications
cover letters, 106
guidelines for, 106
keywords, 106
benefits of, 101-103
career path strategies, 102-103
funding for, 103
versus internships, 101
interviews
expectations after, 108
feedback from, 108
preparation for, 106-108
networking, 104
reference letters, 105
resources for, 110-112
resumes for, 104-105
Robert Wood Johnson Foundation
Action Coalitions, 99
Executive Nurse Fellowship, 99,
110
Health Policy Fellowship, 99, 110
Primary Care Nurse Faculty
Fellowship, 98
Flinter, Margaret (residency program),
100-101
Fraser, Robert *(The Nurse's Social Media
Advantage)*, 75, 124
Fundamental Interpersonal Relations
Orientation-Behavior Assessment
(FIRO-B), 11
future, preferred, 12-15
future of nursing report, 36, 100-101, 141

G

Gallup Honesty and Ethics of Professions
poll, 141, 143
Graduate Record Exam (GRE), 83
graduate school applications. *See also*
recommendations
admissions checklist, 94-95
admissions decision, 93-94
application form, 82
application process, 81
essays
effective essay example, 87-88
ineffective essay example, 88-89
Organized, 86
Professional, 87

Singularity, 86
STOP acronym, 85
Tailored, 86
Graduate Record Exam (GRE), 83
interviews
interview tips, 92-93
preparation for, 91
purposes of, 90
questions to ask MSN and DNP
program interviewers, 92
questions to ask PhD program
interviewers, 92
questions to expect from MSN and
DNP program interviewers, 91
questions to expect from PhD
program interviewers, 91-92
recommendation letters
considerations, 84-85
people to ask, 84
purpose, 83-84
resume, 82
timeline for, 81-95
transcripts, 83
group presentations
attitudes about, 125
guidelines, 126-127
preparation for, 125-126
growth, personal, 10-11
growth, professional, 6, 8-9, 10-11
GRRRR for great listening model, 116-117

H

health disparities, 153
Herrmann Brain Dominance Instrument
(HBDI), 11
higher education applications. *See* graduate
school applications
Hill, Karen, core value statement, 4
Honor Society of Nursing, Sigma Theta Tau
International (STTI), 22, 49
Critical Portfolio, 39
membership requirements, 26
recognition from, 47
resources for internships, 109
humility, 5, 8

I-J

I PASS the BATON, 7
In Real Life (vignettes)
academic program internships, 99-100
advocating for legislation, 130-131, 132
Arroyo, Kate, 64
Belcher, Anne, 114

communication during
recommendation process, 72-73
Connaughton, Mary J., 9
declining request for recommendation,
74
Grigsby, Karen, 26
Hinch, Barbara, 90
job internship/residency, 100
Kirschling, Jane, 12
Masor, Minna B., 32-33, 40-41, 43
Murphy, Marcia, 80
Phillips, Janice, 76
Ridenour, Nancy, 98-99
seeking nominations for recognition,
52
supervision of nurse midwives, 134
Swanson, Barbara, 82
Villarruel, Antonia M., 47
waiving right to see application, 75
Wysocki, Susan, 135-136
Institute of Medicine (IOM)
*The Future of Nursing: Leading
Change, Advancing Health*, 36,
100-101, 141
scholar-in-residence program, 111
internships. *See also* fellowships, residencies
academic program internships, 99-100
applications
cover letters, 106
guidelines for, 106
keywords, 106
benefits of, 101-103
career path strategies, 102-103
versus fellowships, 101
interviews
expectations after, 108
feedback from, 108
portfolios and, 40-41
preparation for, 106-108
job internship/residency, 100
networking, 104
reference letters, 105
residencies, 99, 100-101, 109
resources
nontraditional resources, 111-112
professional organizations, 109
resumes for, 104-105
interviews
graduate school interviews, 90-93
interview tips, 92-93
preparation for, 91
purposes of, 90
questions to ask MSN and DNP
program interviewers, 92

questions to ask PhD program
interviewers, 92
questions to expect from MSN and
DNP program interviewers, 91
questions to expect from PhD
program interviewers, 91-92
internship/fellowship interviews
expectations after, 108
feedback from, 108
preparation for, 106-108
portfolios and, 40-41

K

Kirschling, Jane, core value statement, 5
knowing yourself. *See* self-knowledge
knowledge, 5-6. *See also* self-knowledge

L

latitudes, 118
legislators
nurses as political activists, 145-146
nurses as resources for, 132-134, 163
patient-centered arguments to
influence, 130-131
letters of reference. *See also*
recommendations
graduate school, 83-85
internships/fellowships, 105
lifelong learning, 4
Likert scales, 58, 118
Lindeman, Carol, 12
listening, 116-117
lobbying, 145-146

M

model of sufficiency, in coaching, 15-19
Myers-Briggs Type Indicator (MBTI), 11

N

NAHN (National Association of Hispanic
Nurses), 47
National Library of Medicine, 111
networking, internships and fellowships, 104
Nichols, Barbara
leadership in ANA (American Nurses
Association), 159-161
leadership lessons
creating partnerships, 163
dressing for success, 163
legislative policy, 163
preparation to achieve goal, 162
self-knowledge, 162

strategic thinking, 162
teamwork, 163
minorities in leadership positions,
159-160
nominations for recognition and awards
appropriateness of award, 53
selection of nominators, 54
submission of application, 52, 54-55
timing of submission, 53-54
vignettes, 52
NSNA (National Student Nurses'
Association), 104
nurse educators, 4, 5, 114
nurse empowerment. *See* empowerment of
nurses
nurse residencies, 99, 100-101, 109
nurse-sensitive indicators, 143-144
nursing credentials, 133
nursing organizations
advocacy and, 137-138
benefits of joining, 22-25, 137
checklist, 28
contributions to, 22
focus areas, 24-25
identification of organizations to join,
22, 24-25, 28
involvement in, 137-138
links to lists of nursing organizations,
27
matching personal goals with, 23-25
mission statement, personal, 23
process of joining, 26-27
reflective questions, 24-25
resumes and, 22, 27
sample organizations, 24-25
nursing portfolios. *see* portfolios

O-Q

organizations, professional nursing. *See*
nursing organizations
patient-centered care, 3, 4, 130-131
personal growth, 10-11
persuasion
central *versus* peripheral messages,
119-120
cognitive dissonance theory (CDT),
120-122
definition, 117
elaboration likelihood model (ELM),
118-119
in group presentations, 125-127
latitudes and, 118
Likert scale, 118
social judgment theory and, 118

political action committees (PACs), 146
politics, 145-146
portfolios. *See also* curriculum vitae,
  resumes
    advanced portfolios, 36-38
    artifacts and, 34, 40
    benefits of using, 30, 34, 40-41
    content, 33-37
    creation of professional portfolios
      nursing process and, 41-42
      steps to organize, 42
    versus curriculum vitae, 34
    definition, 30
    designs, 39-40
    electronic portfolios, 39
    examples, 34-36, 38
    intention of, 37
    interviews and, 40-41
    mandatory portfolios, 33
    styles, 39-40
    tab titles, 34-36
    when to use, 40-41
power in nursing actions. *See* empowerment
  of nurses
practice, self-knowledge and, 16-19
presentations to groups. *See* group
  presentations
professional growth. *See* growth,
  professional
professional nursing organizations. *See*
  nursing organizations

R

recognition and awards
    barriers for seeking, 46
    guidelines for fellowships in academies,
      49
    importance to individuals, 46
    importance to institutions, 46
    informal recognition, 46
    nominations for
      appropriateness of award, 53
      selection of nominators, 54
      submission of application, 52,
        54-55
      timing of submission, 53-54
      vignettes, 52
    plans to acquire, 47
      communicating accomplishments,
        50
      meeting people, 50-51
      requesting feedback, 51
    questions to ask, 48

reflection on, 48
self-assessment
    components of, 48
    evaluation of contributions, 48-49
    input from others, 49-50
    personal values, 48
    review of accomplishments, 50
vision for career, 48
recommendations
    applicant's responsibilities in seeking
      asking recommender's permission,
        68
      providing information to
        recommender, 68-69, 71-72
    communication during
      recommendation process, 72-73
    composing own recommendation, 74
    confidentiality and, 74-75
    declining requests for, 64, 73-74
    format of, 58-61
    letters of recommendation
      graduate school, 83-85
      internships/fellowships, 105
    Likert scales, 58
    purpose of, 58
    recommendation letter notes, 71
    Recommender Bank, 61-64
      chart, 62
    review of application guidelines, 65
    Sample Recommendation Form, 59-60
    Sample Recommendation Request, 70
    selection of recommenders
      considerations for, 66-67
      suitability of recommenders, 61,
        63, 65
    social media recommendations, 75
    topics recommenders asked to
      comment on, 63
    waiving right to see application, 75
references. *See* recommendations
reflection, 10, 16-18
repetition, in nonverbal communication, 122
residencies. *See also* fellowships, internships
    definition, 99
    examples, 100-101
    opportunities, 109
resumes. *See also* curriculum vitae,
  portfolios
    components of, 30
    versus curriculum vitae, 32
    definition, 30
    example, 31
    feedback on, 105
    graduate school applications and, 82

for internships and fellowships, 104–105

nursing organizations and, 22, 27

Robert Wood Johnson Foundation
Action Coalitions, 99
Executive Nurse Fellowship, 99, 110
Health Policy Fellowship, 99, 110
Primary Care Nurse Faculty Fellowship, 98

S

school nurses, 132

self-appraisal, 6–7

self-assessment, for recognition and awards
components of, 48
evaluation of contributions, 48–49
feedback, 51, 150
input from others, 49–50
personal values, 48
review of accomplishments, 50

self-awareness, principles of, 16–19

self-confidence, 8, 9

self-knowledge
communication, 6–7
knowledge and skills, 5–6
leadership lessons, Barbara Nichols, 162
model of sufficiency, 15–19
principles of, 16–19
accepting responsibility for yourself, 18–19
aiming for excellence, 17–18
knowing your strengths, 16
seeing yourself clearly, 16–17
reflection and, 16–18
strengths, individual, 8–9, 16
strengths, of others, 10

self-reflection, 10, 16–18

Sigma Theta Tau International (STTI), 22, 49
Critical Portfolio, 39
membership requirements, 26
recognition from, 47
resources for internships, 109

skills, 5–6

SKILLSCOPE, 11

social media, 75, 123–124

strengths, individual, 8–9, 16

strengths, of others, 10

STTI. See Honor Society of Nursing, Sigma Theta Tau International (STTI)

substitution, in nonverbal communication, 123

System for the Multiple Level Observation of Groups (SYMLOG), 11

T

TeamSTEPPS
Ask Me 3 campaign, 7
I PASS the BATON, 7

teamwork, 4, 163

The Future of Nursing: Leading Change, Advancing Health (IOM), 36, 100–101, 141

The Importance of Effective Communication (Wertheim), 122–123

The Nurse's Social Media Advantage (Fraser), 124

Toastmasters, 116

tools
personal and professional growth, 11
TeamSTEPPS, 7

U

United Nations, 111

U.S. Department of Defense and TriService, 7

U.S. Department of Health and Human Services, Agency for Healthcare Research and Quality (AHRQ), 7

U.S. Department of Health and Human Services, Indian Health Service, 7

V

value-based purchasing, 143–144

values, 2–5

Veterans Affairs nursing system, 154

vignettes. See In Real Life (vignettes)

virtual leadership community, 155, 156

volunteer leadership, 151–153, 157–158

W–X–Y–Z

Wertheim, Edward (The Importance of Effective Communication), 122–123

Wharton School of Business, University of Pennsylvania, 111–112

World Health Organization, 111

YMCA programs, 149